This book is dedicated to all the
past, present, and future homeschool teachers
accepting the challenge to make our world a better place.

i

TABLE OF CONTENTS

About the Author, Anita Ottinger. I am the mother of four successfully homeschooled children and 10 grandchildren. I began my homeschool journey reluctantly 20 years ago. With no guidance, I began what would become the adventure of a lifetime, reaping numerous rewards along the way. I want this book to encourage and provide assistance to other homeschool parents so their journey can be one of fun, excitement, and joy. Homeschooling turned out to be the best decision I ever made, and with the help of this book, I hope you can say the same when you complete your destination.

THE REASON FOR HOMESCHOOLING

The American school system today is no longer the thriving institute that used to turn out well-rounded students that led the world in economics, education, power, and religious freedom. Instead, today our country has the lowest educational test scores in the world, and our system of governing is failing us to the point of bankruptcy. Why has the U.S. gone from super power to super dud? What has led us to this great demise?

If we could go back in time and talk to our founding fathers, the answer to this question would be short and sweet. America has taken God out of our school systems and, therefore, out of our country. No one can run this country the way it was intended without God.

At this point in our conversation with our founding fathers someone may ask, "But what about the First Amendment that you all wrote stating separation of church and state." Our founding fathers would then tell us to read the First Amendment again, and we would see that there is no such sentence.

That's right. The statement that has been thrown at us all our lives for the argument of religion in schools, prayer at sporting events, the Ten Commandments in court houses--and so many more injustices on religion--have all been solidified with the statement of "separation of church and state."

There is not a sentence in the American Constitution that states those condemning words; yes, condemning our nation to death and disaster.

What does the First Amendment say? "Congress shall make no law respecting an establishment of religion, or prohibiting the free exercise thereof, or abridging the freedom of speech, or of the press, or the right of the people peaceably to assemble, and to petition the government for a redress of grievances."

That's right; those five words are nowhere to be seen in the Bill of Rights. So, let's look at the First Amendment and see what it does actually say about religion. It refers to government not being able to impose one form of religion or denomination on our country as a national religion as so many of the European countries have done.

Our forefathers knew that without the teachings of the Bible to our youth, our country would become a nation with no character, no morals, and no pride in being free men to pursue our inalienable rights.

So why am I telling you this? We, as homeschoolers, need to teach our children lessons from the Bible every day. We need to fill our nation with honest, happy, fulfilled human beings--human beings that can turn our country back to the super power it once was with God leading the way.

The biggest and most important part of the homeschooling lifestyle is bringing God into our everyday lives. This means to make God the center of our household. Talk to him as you go throughout your day, just as if he were physically standing there with you. Tell him your problems, rejoice with him in your triumphs no matter how big or small, praise him for your blessings, and make sure your children see and hear you doing this.

We were avid church goers before we started homeschooling. After we started homeschooling, we really began learning about God, Jesus, and the Bible as a family in our home. This became a natural part of our lives, and the homeschoolers we hung out with did the same. At first it was surprising how many times a day that the word God,

Lord, and Jesus were spoken in normal conversation about everyday things. I was shocked that this wasn't the case with my church friends. Then one day my son who, at the time was in the sixth grade, out of the blue said, "Mama, it's funny. I've been in church all my life, but since we started homeschooling, I have learned more about God, Jesus, and the Bible than ever before." That was music to my ears, and knowing that, it made me feel so good about our lifestyle change.

So join the homeschool lifestyle, teach the word of God, the Bible, read, pray, and you will have successful children who, one day, will lead our country out of its dark despair, and back into the light of God.

WHY I HOMESCHOOL

My husband came home one day and began to tell me about this radio program he had heard on homeschooling. He was so excited that he actually wrote down the number so we could call and get more information about the subject. He quickly picked up the phone, dialed the number, and asked that information be sent to us.

This whole time I'm thinking, WHO ARE YOU AND WHAT HAVE YOU DONE WITH MY HUSBAND??? My husband is not the type of guy who likes changes, and definitely not as radical as this. Our children were doing fine in school, and we had never even considered homeschooling. Where was he even coming from? I was, to say the least, shocked!

I just laughed at the idea and then looked up into the heavens and said to God, "If you want me to homeschool, you are going to have to connect me with someone who does this to give me advice and the knowledge to get started." I said this to God knowing this was highly unlikely because there was no one around us who homeschooled or even knew anyone that did.

The only homeschool family I ever knew lived in my neighborhood several years ago. Their children were the same ages as mine, and this was a military family. They were a very nice family, but I still thought they were a little strange for not letting their children go to school. I would think how sad it was that they could not socialize with other children.

So now my husband had brought the idea home. My husband, who thought the same way I had for years about the subject, had dropped the homeschool bomb in our house. Only "weirdos" with no socialization skills homeschool; people who live under rocks and are sheltered from the real world; people with only one eye in the middle of their forehead; mutants of the world--these are the types of people that homeschool--unlike us with children who make good grades, earn awards, love school, and are popular with their friends and classmates. The bottom line was: normal people don't homeschool!!

So, after I said my little prayer to God, I totally put the subject out of my head and thought nothing else about it.

The next week I took my children to the Armory in Montgomery for their biweekly gymnastic lessons. I walked into the building and, low and behold, standing there in front of me was my former neighbor who had homeschooled her children. Her family had moved up north four years ago with the military. My heart stopped, my head reeled, and I looked up into the heavens once again and said, "You've got to be kidding me, Lord." I couldn't believe what I was seeing. The only person I had ever known who homeschooled, and one that I hadn't heard from in four years, was standing right in front of me.

Well, I knew then and there what I had to do. God was telling me in no uncertain terms: HOMESCHOOL YOUR CHILDREN!!!!!!!!!!

My first sign was my husband broaching the subject, which was so totally out of character for him, and now this. Wow! I heard him loud and clear. So, reluctantly, I began the process of figuring out what I needed to do to homeschool my children.

To do this legally, you must have your children enrolled in a "Cover School." This is a place that keeps records of you and sends the public school system your enrollment information showing that you are homeschooling and your child is not just playing hooky.

A cover school is also a support group where homeschool families can get together and do fun things such as clubs for the kids, mom's night out, fieldtrips, P.E., and park days. For the children who are in junior high and high school, some cover groups have classes once a week to enrich the learning experience they are getting at home and sometimes teach things that moms can't teach.

There was a network of homeschooling people and organizations that I didn't even know existed; and, believe it or not, the people who participated in this network were "normal." Or, maybe I should say "better than normal," because these people really had their heads on straight and knew a little more about living a good life than the rest of us.

They had their priorities in the right order and really enjoyed their family and friends and day-to-day living. It was like they had broken the code, figured out the puzzle, and knew the combination to what the rest of the world was looking for.

Now that we had halfway figured out what we were doing, our kids finished the school year, and the next fall they stayed home. My son was in the sixth grade, my daughter was in the fourth, my youngest son was in the second, and my youngest daughter was three years old.

My kids didn't complain at all when I told them we were homeschooling, which was another miracle from God. When they or anyone else asked me why we were homeschooling, I would tell them, "Because God told me to." When God tells you to do something, you do it. When all was said and done, I can honestly say it was the best decision that we ever made. The biggest lesson we learned in all of this is that if you do what God wants you to do, he will bless your life over and over again.

UNSCHOOLING

There is a lot of talk in the homeschooling community about traditional methods of teaching versus the "unschooling" method. I can honestly say I did a little bit of both. That is the great thing about homeschooling--you can teach your children in a way that fits into their learning styles and your lifestyle.

What is unschooling you ask?? The best way I can describe it is to allow your children to choose what they are interested in knowing and then help them find the right resources and supplies to immerse themselves into a true and honest mode of learning; a mode that does not involve a lot of teaching on your part but with only minimal support and help as you see fit.

For example, suppose your child is really into cooking. They can look up recipes online or in a cookbook. They can call or write grandma and their aunts and collect favorite family recipes to be used in making and publishing a family cookbook. They can take pictures of the ingredients and finished recipes. As they cook and measure the ingredients, they can learn about fractions and how combining different ingredients will cause certain chemical reactions. This, in turn, can lead into growing their own fresh ingredients to make healthier dishes.

When they plant their own garden, they will learn about plants, seeds, soil, composting, worms, and organic growing methods. The list goes on and on. They can learn about the origins of different foods and how different cultures cook with them.

They can make a grocery list and find coupons for the items. They can go to the grocery store with a certain amount of money and figure out--after the sale and using a coupon--how much the product will cost and if they have enough money to pay for it.

Your child can learn how health and food go hand-in-hand; what's good for your body and what's not; how processing food with chemicals is unhealthy; how to read a label to know what to avoid and what is good for you.

I could keep on going, but I think you get the point. With just this one hobby your child can learn science, math, language arts, geography, history, photography, and publishing. Interest in these activities will, in turn, lead to interest in other things, and the process continues.

You and your child should set goals for the day, week, or month and try to meet these goals. This is a good way to stay on track and keep up with what has been done. Also, it will give you a heads-up on what you might need to have on hand for all of their projects and interests.

The Do's and Don'ts of the Homeschooling Lifestyle

DO:

• Remember, you are not in public or private school anymore.

• Be creative when choosing curriculum.

• Make learning a part of everything you do.

• Read, read, read, with your kids--anything and everything.

• Have hands-on learning activities included in your schooling.

• Use car travel as a time to learn spelling words, reading, reviewing the day's lessons, learning a foreign language, and listening to books on tape.

• Make your house a home.

• Limit TV.

• Do remember that the outdoor spaces can be special. Get outside and enjoy nature!

• Use fresh ingredients when cooking.

• Get everybody in the family involved in cooking.

- Eat together at the table.
- Make meal time an event!
- Enjoy all kinds of different music in your home.
- Talk with your neighbors.
- Spend time with your loved ones, family, and friends.
- Skip the gym and grow a vegetable and/or flower garden.
- Give your children responsibilities around the house and yard.
- Give to your favorite charities.
- Make God the center of your family and life.
- Ask God to guide you as you teach your children and to bless them in this endeavor.
- Make life an adventure!!

<u>DON'T:</u>

- Stick your kid in front of a textbook and call it schooling.
- Be on a strict time schedule.
- Forget to make everyday activities a learning experience.
- Lose sight of why you are homeschooling.
- Surround your kids or yourself with electronics.
- Text.
- Talk on your cell phone and disturb people around you.
- Involve your kids in so many activities that they don't have time for playing, family, and friends.
- Buy your kids too many toys.
- Forget to talk to God every day.
- Forget to thank God for your life and everything in it.
- Dismiss your house as just a place to stay.
- Forget to stop and smell the roses.
- Put TV in your child's room.
- Eat prepackaged food.

TO WORK OR NOT TO WORK; THAT IS THE QUESTION

Throughout history, there has been the question of whether working outside the home is God's plan for women. Women of the Bible had many roles, but their number one priority as wives and mothers was their family and home.

My favorite verses about women in the Bible are Proverbs 31:10-31. These verses describe the woman we would love to aspire to be. She is Godly, hard-working, an entrepreneur, an excellent housewife, and mother. This lady is a mixture of Martha Stewart, Mother Teresa, and Carol Brady. Wow, she is the perfect woman.

Of course we know that no one can be perfect, but what makes us productive and happy and good wives and mothers is the desire to be perfect, the desire to have a great relationship with our husbands, the desire to raise well-rounded children, the desire to have a beautiful, happy, and healthy household; and, of course, the core of it all, have a great relationship with God.

I think the reason most verses in the Bible depict women as stay-at-home moms and wives is because life just works better this way. Running a household is one of the most important jobs in the world. Today's society, as a whole, has diminished this role and so has diminished the family as God had intended it to be.

Today people value having "stuff," and lots of it, and having careers as the number one priority in life. We forget to stop and smell the roses and enjoy life anymore.

Our families are being raised by strangers, and our homes are just a place to lay our head at night. Could this be why society has come to be what it is: cold, uncaring, and tired. We have taken the most important part of the equation out of life, God, Family, and Home.

I have been a stay-at-home mom and wife my entire marriage. My husband and I have occasionally had trouble making ends meet, but for the most part, thanks to God, we have had everything we ever wanted plus much, much, more. I, like the lady in the Bible verse, have had some odd jobs here and there, but not one of them ever took time away from my family. My motto is, do your best at what God has intended for you to do, and you will be blessed over and over again.

People like to complain or make excuses for how the Bible says that we should live, but when you get right down to it, the Bible is the "how to" book for a happy and healthy life. God only gives us rules to keep us healthy and happy. Everything that's in the Bible is for our own good. He created us, and he wants us to have the most perfect existence that we can have on this Earth. He doesn't give us rules to keep us from having fun but to enhance our lives and make us joyful.

So, as wives and mothers, let's take back the most important job on Earth: raising our children and taking care of our husbands and households. Let's hold this position high and make it a priority in this world once again.

I truly believe that if we do, our world would do a 365-degree turn, and we would see the return of civilization as we once knew it. There would be less crime, divorce, drug, and alcohol abuse; and people would truly feel a serenity that has been missing from their lives. This is exactly what our home school revolution is all about: Living the wonderful lives God has given us and living it to the fullest!!

SOCIALIZING CHILDREN: THE GREAT MYTH

Socializing your baby and toddler has become an obsession with today's parents. Society has told us that if we don't put our child in a preschool or mom's-day-out, the child will be socially stunted and ignorant. Of course, as parents, we want the best for our child. We want them to be smart, well-rounded people so we listen to the demands of society, as we have all been programmed to do, instead of doing our own research on the subject; so what happens is just the opposite of our loving intent.

I am aware that in some situations both mother and father need to work in order to make ends meet, but in many more cases a couple could easily downsize so that one of the parents could stay home to rear the children.

Research after research has been done on this myth, and the outcome is always the same. If a group of children are put in a room together with only one or two adults, the opposite happens. They become emotionally insecure unhappy children with issues of low self-esteem and behavioral problems.

My two daughters and I have all worked in different daycares and preschools at one time or another. We agree wholeheartedly that this is the last place on earth we would put our children.

In my experience I've worked with toddlers and kindergartners at two different locations. The toddlers constantly fought for my attention and, as in nature, (survival of the fittest) the strongest and meanest child got what he wanted while the others suffered. I had a bird's-eye view of the socialization process, and let me tell you: It's appalling.

If I sat on the floor, all the toddlers in the room lunged for me demanding my attention. They cried and fought to be the one in my lap, and when my lap was running over with children, the weakest ones were left to cry on the floor. No, I'm not making this up. One or two ladies cannot supply a room full of toddlers with the attention they need. It's impossible.

Not only does the child have no feelings of self-worth but also anxiety and depression; the so-called socialization skills they are getting are of wild animals in the zoo. I know this is strong language, but it needs to be said. The toddlers learn how to be manipulative, how to fight, and how to be loud and obnoxious. What they are learning is how to survive.

I don't know about you but I don't want my toddler learning about survival and having to fight for love and attention. As a socialized adult, I don't recall that fighting and manipulating people are high on the list of being a well-rounded, good person.

My oldest daughter worked in a church daycare and preschool in the baby room and toddler room. She said that a prerequisite to putting your child in a day care should be that the mother have to stay one full day before leaving her child. If they did that, daycares would become obsolete. She said no one would leave their child in that kind of environment day in and day out. My youngest daughter has also worked in a daycare, and she now totally agrees with this assessment.

How then should we socialize our children? God's intent was for a mother to raise a child. There is no better place than in the home around the family for a child to get socialized. There a child finds love. No one at a daycare truly loves your child. They might like them, but they do not have the nurturing instinct of a mother who truly loves them. A child finds security, self-worth, and room to become themselves in a time and manner that are conducive to their needs and personality.

If you think a preschool is the only way to prepare your children for kindergarten, think again. It's not rocket science that they are teaching your kids. It's colors, letters, and numbers; things that we all know. Don't you think you can teach your child these simple lessons?

In the 1980s daycare centers became the norm in America. Mothers worked because they wanted their children to have everything they needed and wanted. Do you know the most important thing a child needs and wants? Their mother!!! Today the majority of American families have their children in preschools and daycares.

The teens of the 2000 era were the first group of teens that were predominantly raised in a daycare. Is it just me or has anyone else noticed that these children are so lacking in social skills that it is scary? Most teens will not even look an adult in the face when speaking to them, if they speak to them at all. These kids can text but that's about it, and that is not a social skill.

The teen dating ritual is practically obsolete because today they don't know how to communicate with one another. It's scary, people! These kids are going to be running our country soon.

I read an article about making your decision to work or stay at home. There were all kinds of reasons to work and reasons to stay at home, but what shocked me about the article was that the reasons were all based around the mom and what made her happy. There were no reasons based on the child and what was best for them.

So let me just end with this statement. Socializing is a crock. Do your research, and you'll find out for yourself!!!

THE POWER OF PRAYER

What is a Christian and what does it entail? A Christian is someone who loves God with all their soul and all their heart and all their mind. Christianity, when you get right down to it, has nothing to do with religion, church, doctrine, or ceremony. The bottom line on Christianity is believing in and loving God and Jesus Christ and having a real relationship with them.

Some say, "Oh, I go to church every time the doors are open"; therefore, making them a Christian. But what do they do at home, in the car, or while they are working? Do they have a day-to-day relationship with God? Becoming and being a Christian is one of the easiest tasks on Earth. Believe, love, and have an on-going relationship with him every day.

So what do I mean by an on-going relationship? Let's look at it this way. If you talked to your spouse for thirty minutes a week, do you think you would have any kind of relationship? NO; you would hardly know each other. God, like anyone else in your life, wants to be a part of it. He wants to know when you are happy, sad, worried, or just plain bored. He wants to know all your dreams for the future, and he wants to revel in your accomplishments.

When you wake up in the morning, do you ignore your spouse and children, or do you say, "Good morning" (even if you are not a morning person) when you pass them in the hall? More times than not you say good morning or at least grunt at them.

Well, God wants you to do the same for him; maybe not the grunt, but that would be better than nothing. When you go through your day, talk to him just as if he were standing in front of you. Tell him how your day is going, what problems you are having, or thank him for the beauty around you, your children, your life. Thank him for letting your newborn spit up on you instead of some day care worker. Talk to him before you eat and before you go to bed. Talk to him as a couple or a family. Have some quiet time and discuss the day's topics with him.

Can't find any place to have quiet time? I know the feeling. The best place I have found--as a mom--is, believe it or not, on the toilet. That's right; I said toilet. Even then, sometimes that's not private. I love the little fingers sticking under the door. Then I laugh and thank him for the opportunity and blessing of being a stay-at-home mom. He understands, trust me.

When you have an on-going relationship with God, your life runs smoother; you are a happier, more upbeat person; your problems become less, and blessings abound.

Now let's talk about trust. Trusting in God takes a lot of faith. What is faith, you ask. Believing God will do something for you, no matter what, and believing in something you cannot see or touch. Your children have faith that you will always be there for them and will never let anything bad happen to them. They truly believe this, and they don't even have to think about it. This is the kind of faith we should have in God. If you truly believe he can do anything, he will. Ask for what you need, and he will give it to you. Seriously, he will answer your prayers. Believe in him, and it will happen.

Sometimes things in this world will not go exactly how you think or want them to go because we live in an imperfect society, but God will provide your needs, and He wants to keep you safe and happy. He wants the best for you, and all you need to do is believe this.

Sometimes the things you pray for may come to you in an unexpected way; but remember, God thinks of everything and knows the best way to answer your prayers.

Sometimes he may even say no because he knows that is the best thing for you.

Christians really need to harness the power of prayer. It is amazing and a life changing miracle that can happen every day. The power of prayer is real, and a miracle is out there for everyone if you just believe.

Having an on-going relationship with God is the first step in realizing just how real and powerful and loving he is. When you have this relationship, your whole life will change, and things that you thought could never happen become a day-to-day miracle. You begin to look at life and realize how powerful God is and how wonderful it is having him on your side. Life is truly awesome when you have this relationship with him. He is really, really, really there for you every step of the way.

If more people had this relationship, the world could do miraculous things. So talk to God and Jesus all the time. Teach your children to do the same. Do this and see how wonderful and fulfilling your life can truly be.

LET'S GET ORGANIZED

Homeschooling is a new way of life and a new beginning for your family! It's time to shed those sluggish ways and start fresh with a clear mind and new ideas.

Organization is the key to success in everything we do, so let's get started with some new ideas that can make our life easier and more productive. Being organized can be simpler than you think.

Keep a calendar in a convenient spot in your home so every member of your family can stay informed about what's happening on a day-to-day basis. I like to color code my calendar by giving each member of the family a color of their own. With just a quick glance, they can see what their day holds. Also, it is good to have a color just for home schooling events. On the weekend, take a few minutes to fill out your calendar for the next week.

This way nothing sneaks up on you, and you are prepared for almost anything.

Organizing your lesson plans can take over your life if you let it. I like to have a general idea of what I am teaching for the next few months and then break it down monthly. Fill the house with the right books, science supplies, craft supplies, posters, charts, etc. that you and your children will need to have a fun and rewarding month.

Have a basket or box with items that relate to each subject you are teaching and that are easily accessible to your children. Keep the books you are using in places where your child will notice them. Put them on the coffee table, on the bedside table, in the play room, in the car, and don't forget the most important reading room in the house--the bathroom. My children have read more in that room than any other room in the house. Talk about multi-tasking! Having the books out like this versus put away on a book shelf will encourage your child to pick one up and discover it.

Keep a box of science supplies in your child's reach so he/she can explore and create on their own. For instance, if you are studying plants, fill your box with a magnifying glass, seeds, trowel, an egg carton for starting seeds, a bag of soil, small flower pots, and paints to decorate the pots with. Also, pictures of plants that they can color or paint and identify, coffee filters for making into flowers and butterflies, and a throw-away camera for taking pictures. There are endless possibilities.

For history, do the same. For instance, if you are studying early American history, put Lincoln logs or popsicle sticks in the box for building log cabins. Put clothes, long skirts, aprons, hats, and vests in it so they can play dress up. Put your imagination to work so your kids can use theirs. When your environment is filled with items and activities that are easily accessible, learning can be integrated into everyday life and not forced on them for a certain number of hours each day. Immerse your life into learning.

Okay, you've got your activities on the calendar and your lessons planned and organized, but what about your household chores. How do you keep your house clean and organized while you home school and play chauffer to the many activities your family is involved in?

Keeping things picked up is half the battle. If you walk into your house and there are objects strewn all over, it is hard to concentrate or feel relaxed. When things are put away, your stress level shrinks considerably. Every day for 15 to 20 minutes give you and your kids one or two rooms each to de-clutter. Put the dirty clothes in the hamper, the clean clothes in the drawers and closet, the toys in the toy box, the trash in the trash can, and the dishes in the sink or dishwasher.

Now that you can actually find the room, let's get down to the nitty-gritty such as cleaning bathrooms, dusting, vacuuming, sweeping, mopping and all the fun stuff we love doing. NOT!! I like to make a weekly list for these things. This way I don't feel overwhelmed; I don't forget anything; and best of all I get to scratch items off my list, and this makes me feel that I am accomplishing my goal. Here is a list you can copy and use in your own home.

Check List

Monday: Load of laundry; dust.

Tuesday: Load of laundry; clean bathroom sinks, tubs and toilets.

Wednesday: Load of laundry; clean mirrors and glass surfaces and change the sheets.

<u>Thursday</u>: Load of laundry; sweep and mop.

<u>Friday</u>: Load of laundry; vacuum.

By following this list, your house will be clean, and you will have spent minimal time each day getting chores done; and be sure your children stay involved.

Last, but not least, I will touch on organization. If the house is organized, it can almost clean itself. It may take you a few weekends to organize every room in your house, but trust me; this is the key to less stress, more relaxation, and a better life style. Clean out drawers, closets, cabinets, laundry room, and storage room. Remember: "Less is more." Get rid of items that you haven't used or worn in the past year. Give them to your friends or charity or have a yard sale and earn some extra money.

Put half of your children's toys in a box that you can store away. Every three months or so, swap the toys out, and your children will feel like they have new ones. Too many toys are a distraction and will keep your kids from focusing on a particular activity and, therefore, are very unproductive.

Use inexpensive plastic containers and label them to keep things in the correct place. For smaller children who can't read, label your containers with pictures. If your children know where to put items, cleanup is fast and easy. To keep your house organized, take 15 minutes a day to go through a drawer or a cabinet, and you will continually "have a place for everything and everything in its place."

To sum it all up: It should take approximately 30 minutes a weekend to fill out your calendar, one morning a month to get books out and items together for your science and history boxes, approximately 15 minutes a day to tidy your rooms, and one hour a day for chores, and 15 minutes a day to keep organized. Total for cleaning, organizing, and doing laundry each day: one hour and 30 minutes.

Now remember, these are approximate times--and some days may vary--but if you will do these things, I guarantee your house will stay clean, and life will be much more enjoyable.

HOWEVER, remember that the home-schooling life is a challenge, and there may be a new adventure or setback. Don't let it throw you if you don't keep to a strict schedule today because "tomorrow is a new day," so just remember to go with the flow. This could have been the day your child had a real breakthrough or this could have been a "memory making" day!!

WHAT MY CHILD NEEDS TO KNOW
FOR
KINDERGARTEN

<u>Science</u>: Plants and Animals--life cycles and characteristics; example: feathers, roots.

Seasons and weather.

The Human Body--scences, parts.

Measurements and Motion--magnets (push and pull) and comparing objects by weight and size.

Famous Scientists--George Washington Carver, Jane Goodall, Wright Brothers.

<u>Social Studies</u>: Be familiar with events and people associated with U.S. holidays.

Put days, weeks, and months in proper order.

Recognize the flag and Statue of Liberty.

Know that the world is divided into different countries and the similarities and differences between the cultures.

Show the differences between land and water on a globe.

Know that the U.S. is divided into States.

Reading: Know how books are read--front cover to back cover, top of page to bottom, from left to right.

Recognize the cover, title page, and table of contents.

Read, read, read to your children.

Know the sounds of each letter and also the blends, such as "ph makes the f sound."

Know long vowel and short vowel sounds.

Read one syllable words (cat, dog).

Read one syllable rhyming words (hat, cat, mat).

Be able to retell a story and identify the characters, setting, and events of that story.

Writing: Write lower and upper case letters.

Write their name.

Spell (consonant-vowel-consonant) words such as bat, cat, fan, ham, sad, etc.

Let them tell you a story and you write it down.

Technology: Know simple computer skills; how to work a mouse and navigate a child's web site.

Math: Count to 100.

Count by fives to 100.
Count by tens to 100.

Identify numbers up to 20.

Identify shapes.

Identify and count coins.

Group objects by color, shape, and size.

Understand a calendar--yesterday, today, and tomorrow.

Know about the big hand and little hand on a clock and be able to tell time to the hour.

Introduce addition and subtraction. Example: If you had five apples and you ate one, how many would you have left?

<u>Miscellaneous</u>: Know address and phone number.

Know how to use "911."

Know eight basic colors--red, yellow, blue, green, orange, black, white, and pink.

Cut with scissors along a line.

Follow directions.

Pay attention for 15 to 20 minutes.

Sight Words for Kindergarten

- all
- am
- an
- and
- are
- as
- at
- at
- ate
- away
- be
- big
- black
- blue
- brown
- but
- came
- can
- come
- did

- do
- down
- eat
- eight
- find
- five
- for
- four
- get
- go
- good
- green
- has
- have
- he
- her
- here
- hers
- him
- his

- in
- into
- is
- it
- like
- little
- look
- make
- me
- must
- my
- new
- nine
- no
- not
- now
- of
- on
- one
- orange
- our
- out
- play

- please
- pretty
- purple
- red
- ride
- run
- said
- say
- see
- seven
- she
- six
- small
- so
- soon
- ten
- that
- the
- there
- they
- this
- three
- to

- too
- two
- under
- up
- want
- was
- we
- well
- went

- what
- white
- who
- why
- will
- with
- year
- yellow
- yes

BOOKS FOR YOUR KINDERGARTNER

"Dick and Jane" Readers.

"Bob Books" (readers).

"Biscuit Phonics Fun" by Alyssa Satin Capucilli and Pat Schories.

"Biscuit Story Book Collection" by Alyssa Satin Capucilli.

"Amelia Bedelia Books" by Herman Parish.

NOTE: Kindergartners may also use the book section under First Grade Books.

WHAT MY CHILD NEEDS TO KNOW
FOR FIRST GRADE

<u>Science</u>: Oceans and sea life--waves, currents, coral reefs, sea animals, sea plants.

<u>The Human Body</u>: Systems, and how to care for your body.

<u>Matter</u>: The three states of matter--solid, liquid, gas (ice/solid, water/liquid, steam/gas).

<u>Measurement</u>: Temperature and how it's measured.

<u>Intro to Electricity</u>: Electrical currents and circuits, batteries.

<u>Magnets</u>.

<u>Sound</u>: Vibrating objects produce sound, and sound travels.

<u>Social Studies</u>: Identify community, states, countries, continents, and oceans on a map.

Make and use a simple map. Know directions.

Compare different cultures and how they live.

Know the ways of an earlier time, (pioneer, Roman, Egyptian, etc).

Reading: Read out loud.

Read one- and two-syllable words.

Identify beginning, middle, and ending sounds.

Writing: Write a complete sentence with correct punctuation and capitalization.

Write every day--journal, short stories, poems, letters, songs.

Spelling: Weekly spelling list. Four letter words; words with silent "e" at the end. Color (blue, green, red) number words one through twelve.

Technology: Use word processing program.

Math: Patterns and shapes.

Count to a hundred by 2's.

Addition up to 20.

Two-digit number problems.

Subtraction from 20 and down.

Word problems.

Add different combinations of coins.

Learn to measure using inches, cups, and quarts.

Tell time to the hour and half hour.

Be able to do mental math.

BOOKS FOR YOUR FIRST GRADER

"The Boy Who Loved Words" by Roni Schotter.

"Edward and the Pirates" by David McPhail.

"Max's Words" by Kate Banks (get excited about writing).

"You Read to Me, I'll Read to You: Very Short Fairy Tales to Read Together" by Mary Ann Heberman.

"The Apple Pie That Papa Baked" by Lauren Thompson (fun science).

"Charlotte's Web" by E.B. White.

"The Hundred Dresses" by Eleanor Estes (learn compassion).

"Mr. Popper's Penguines" by Richard and Florence Atwater.

"How I Became a Pirate" by Melinda Long.

"Mind Your Manners, B. B. Wolf" by Judy Sierra (a fun lesson in manners).

"Why Don't You Get a Horse, Sam Adams" by Jean Fritz.

"George Washington's Cows" by David Small.

"The Giant Hug" by Sandra Horning.

"Smash! Mash! Crash! There Goes the Trash!" by Barbara Odanaka.

"Washday on Noah's Ark" by Glen Rounds.

"Ballerina Girl (My First Reader Series)" by Kirsten Hall.

"Museum ABC" by Metropolitan Museum of Art (has actual paintings in it).

"The Shape Game" by Anthony Browne. (Teach your kids to look for the story and details in a painting.)

"The Rookie Biography Series" by Nancy Polette.

"Picasso and Minou" by P. L. Maltbie.

"The Pilgrim's First Thanksgiving" by Ann McGovern.

"The Nature Treasury: A first Look at the Natural World" by Lizann Flatt.

"Uneversaurus" by Aidan Potts (a book about dinosaurs.)

"Why? The Best Ever Question and Answer Book About Nature, Science, and the World Around You" by Catherine Ripley.

"Why Do Leaves Change Color?" by Betsy Maestro.

"Science Verse" by Jan Scieszka.

"A Pioneer Sampler--One in a Series" by Barbara Greenwood.

"A Child's History of the World" by V.M. Hillyer.

"What Your First Grader Needs to Know" by E.D. Hirsch.

"Where Do I Live?" by Neil Chesanow.

"Full House: An Invitation to Fractions" by Dayle Ann Dodds.

"If You Were A Fraction" by Trisha Speed Shaskan.

"Math For All Seasons" by Greg Tang.

"Ray's Arithmetic Series" by Joseph Ray. (Written in the 1870's, it teaches children math in a way that they can apply in real life situations.)

"I Wonder Why Greeks Built Temples: and Other Questions About Ancient Greece" by Fiona MacDonald (from the series "I Wonder Why").

"Classical Kids: An Activity Guide to Life in Ancient Greece and Rome (A Kid's Guide Series)" by Laurie Carlson.

"I Wonder Why Romans Wore Togas" by Fiona MacDonald.

"Tiger, Tiger" by Lynne Reid Banks (historical fiction depicting Ancient Rome).

"Where Do Chicks Come From? (Lets-Read-and-Find-Out-Level 1)" by Amy E. Sklansky and Pam Paparone.

"The Chick That Wouldn't Hatch" by Claire Daniel and Lisa Campbell Ernst (a reader for ages 5-7).

"Out and About at the Dairy Farm" by Andy Murphy and Anne McMullen.

"A Fairy in a Dairy" by Lucy Noland and Laura J. Bryant.

"The Year at Maple Hill Farm" by Alice Provensen and Martin Provensen.

"What's Under the Sea? (Starting Point Science)" by Sophy Tahta and Stuart Trotter.

"The Magic School Bus on the Ocean Floor" by Joanna Cole and Bruce Degen.

"What Lives in a Shell? (Let's-Read-and-Find-Out-Science 1)" by Kathleen Weidner Zoehfeld and Helen K. Davie.

"An Octopus is Amazing (Let's-Read-and-Find-Out-Science 2)" by Patricia Lauber and Holly Keller.

"Ocean Soup: Tide-Pool Poems" by Stephen R. Swinburne and Bruce Hiscock.

"See Inside Your Body" by Katie Daynes and Colin King.

"Me and My Amazing Body" by Joan Sweeney and Anette Cable.

"Inside Your Outside: All About the Human Body (Cat in the Hat's Learning Library)" by Tish Rabe and Aristides Ruiz.

"The Magic School Bus Jumping into Electricity" by The Magic School Bus.

"Our 50 States" by Lynne Cheney and Robin Preiss Glasser.

"What Is the World Made Of? All About Solid, Liquids, and Gases (Let's-Read-and-Find-Out Science, stage 2)" by Kathleen Weidner Zoehfeld and Paul Meisel.

"Sound All Around (Let's-Read-and-Find-Out Science, Stage 2)" by Wendy Pfeffer and Holly Keller.

"You Can't Smell a Flower With Your Ear" by Joanna Cole and Mavis Smith.

"Magnets (All Aboard Science Reader)" by Ann Schreiber and Adrian C. Sinnott.

"Amazing Magnetism (Magic School Bus Chapter Book #12)" by Rebecca Carmi and John Speirs.

"On a Beam of Light: A Story of Albert Einstein" by Jennifer Berne and Vladimir Radunsky.

"The Boy Who Loved Math: The Improbable Life of Paul Erdos" by Deborah Heiligman and LeUyen Pham.

"Bed Time Math" by Laura Overdeck and Jim Paillot.

"Your Fantastic Elastic Brain" by JoAnn Deak, Ph.D, and Sarah Ackerley.

"Seaman's Journal: On the Trail With Lewis and Clark" by Patti Reeder Eubank.

"The Life and Times of the Ant" by Charles Micucci.

"Secrets of the Garden: Food Chains and the Food Web in Our Backyard" by Kathleen Weidner Zoehfeld and Priscilla Lamont.

"Roots, Shoots, Buckets and Boots: Gardening Together with Children" by Sharon LoveJoy.

"Compost Stew" by Mary Mckenna Siddals.

"An Earthworm's Life (Nature Upclose)" by John Himmelman.

WHAT MY CHILD NEEDS TO KNOW
FOR SECOND GRADE

Science: The Cycle of Life.
Seasons.
Human Body--systems, nutrition, organs, tissues and cells.
Insects.
Electricity and magnetism.
Sun, Moon, planets, and stars.

Social Studies: Maps, states, continents, oceans, seas. Learn patriotic songs such as Star Spangled Banner, America the Beautiful, My Country Tis of Thee.

Learn the Pledge of Allegiance.

Reading: Read chapter books.
Know how to use a Table of Contents and an index.
Learn to do research using informational books and the internet.

<u>Language Arts</u>: Know prefixes and suffixes and their meanings.

>Plurals.

>Compound words.

>Antonyms and synonyms.

>Nouns and verbs.

<u>History</u>: American history.

>World history.

>Government--types of government, democracy, communism, socialism, etc.

<u>Math</u>: Adding and subtracting up to three numbers (4+5+3=).

>Adding and subtracting two digit numbers (25+45=).

>Counting numbers up to 1000.

>Counting money. Add and subtract money with decimal points (4.50+5.75=).

>Word problems.

>Place value--1879; the one is in the thousand's place, the eight is in the hundred's place, the seven is in the ten's place, and the nine is in the one's place.

Know the symbols--less than ≤, greater than ≥ and equal to =

Start memorizing multiplication tables.

Tell time with a real clock.

AM and PM.

Roman numerals.

Measure length.

Introduce fractions.

BOOKS FOR YOUR SECOND GRADER

"Science Verse" by John Scieszka (habitat stories and the animals that live there).

"The Flyer Flew! The Invention of the Airplane" by Lee Sullivan.

"Smart About Series" by Laura Driscol.

"What Presidents Are Made Of" by Hanoch Piven.

"It's Disgusting and We Ate It" (unique historical facts from around the world) by James Solheim.

"On the Mayflower" by Kate Waters.

"The Story of the Pilgrims" by Katherine Ross.

"My Senator and Me" by Edward M. Kennedy.

"Compost, by Gosh" by Michelle Eva Portman.

"Recycle! A Handbook for Kids" by Gail Gibbons.

"The Busy Body Book: A Kid's Guide to Fitness" by Lizzy Rockwell.

"Ben and Me" by Robert Lawson (a book about Ben Franklin told by a mouse).

"A Child's History of the World" by V.M. Hillyer.

"What Your Second Grader Needs to Know" by E.D. Hirsch.

"Math Books" by Greg Tang.

"A Very Improbable Story: A Math Adventure" by Edward Einhorn.

"Brian Cleary's Language Arts Series."

"Ray's Arithmetic Series" by Joseph Ray. (Written in the 1870s, these books teach children math in a way that they can apply it in real life situations.)

"Blackbeard the Pirate King" by J. Patrick Lewis.

"Frog Friends (Animal Ark Pets #15)" by Ben M. Baglio. (One in a series, these are good readers for 2nd and 3rd grade.)

"Why Frogs Are Wet (Let's-Read-and-Find-Out 2)" by Judy Hawes and Mary Ann Fraser.

"Tale of a Tadpole" by Karen Wallace (DK Readers--good readers, this is one in a series; great pictures explaining tadpoles and life cycles.)

"Where Butterflies Grow" by Joanne Ryder and Lynne Cherry (beautiful illustrations).

"Gotta Go Gotta Go (Sunburst Books)" by Sam Swope and Sue Riddle (about the migration of the Monarch to Mexico).

"The Reasons For the Seasons" by Gail Gibbons.

"Learning About the Changing Seasons" by Heidi Gold-Dworkin and Robert K. Ullman.

"In the Town All Year Round" by Rotraut Berner.

"The Year at Maple Hill Farm" by Alice Provensen and Martin Provensen.

"Chicken Soup with Rice: A Book of Months" by Maurice Sendak.

"My First Human Body Book (Dover Children's Science Books)" by Patricia J. Wynne and Donald M. Silver.

"My Body (Science Books)" by Patty Carratello.

"Me and My Amazing Body" by Joan Sweeney and Anette Cable.

"Inside Your Outside: All About the Human Body (Cat in the Hat's Learning Library)" by Tish Rabe and Aristides Ruiz.

"The Magic School Bus: A Journey Into the Human Body" by The Young Scientists Club.

"The Honey Makers" by Gail Gibbons.

"Are You a Bee? (Backyard Books)" by Judy Allen (The "Are You a_____" series: spider, dragonfly, ladybug, ant, snail.

"The Magic School Bus Inside a Beehive" by Joanna Cole and Bruce Degen.

"Velma Gratch and the Way Cool Butterfly" by Alan Madison and Kevin Hawkes.

"Switch on, Switch Off (Let's-Read-and-Find-Out 2)" by Melvin Berger and Carolyn Croll.

"Charged Up: The Story of Electricity (Science Works)" by Jacqui Bailey and Matthew Lilly.

"The Magic School Bus Jumping into Electricity" by the Magic School Bus.

"The Big Dipper (Let's-Read-and-Find-Out Science 1)" by Franklyn M. Branley and Molly Cox.

"What's Out There? A Book about Space (Reading Railroad)" by Lynn Wilson and Paige Billin-Frye.

"Astronaut Handbook" by Meghan McCarthy.

"National Geographic Kid's Big Book of Space" by Catherine D. Hughes and David A. Aguilar.

"National Geographic Readers: Planets" by Elizabeth Carney.

"Our 50 States" by Lynne Cheney and Robin Preiss Glasser.

"America: A Patriotic Primer" by Lynne Cheney and Robin Preiss Glasser.

"Land of the Pilgrim's Pride (Ellis the Elephant)" by Callista Gingrich and Susan Arciero.

"Sweet Land of Liberty (Ellis the Elephant)" by Callista Gingrich and Susan Arciero.

"Roots, Shoots, Buckets, and Boots: Gardening Together with Children" by Sharon LoveJoy.

"Compost Stew" by Mary Mckenna Siddals.

"An Earthworm's Life (Nature Upclose)" by John Himmelman.

"Secrets of the Garden: Food Chains and the Food Web in Our Backyard" by Kathleen Weidner Zoehfeld and Priscilla Lamont.

"Bedtime Math" by Laura Overdeck and Jim Paillot.

"Your Fantastic Elastic Brain" by JoAnn Deak Ph.D and Sarah Ackerley.

"On a Beam of Light: A Story of Albert Einstein" by Jennifer Berne and Vladimir Radunsky.

"The Boy Who Loved Math: The Improbable Life of Paul Erdos" by Deborah Heiligman and LeUyen Pham.

"Trail of Tears (Step-Into-Reading, Step 5)" by Joseph Bruchac.

"Seaman's Journal: On the Trail With Lewis and Clark" by Patti Reeder Eubank.

"The Life and Times of the Ant" by Charles Micucci.

WHAT MY CHILD NEEDS TO KNOW
FOR THIRD GRADE

<u>Science</u>: Classification of animals--vertebrate, invertebrate.

The human body--sight and hearing.

Electricity.

Gravity.

Solar system.

Forces and motion--how and why objects move.

<u>Social Studies</u>: Maps--longitude and latitude, prime meridian, equator, North Pole, South Pole.

Ecosystems.

<u>History</u>:   American History.

World History.

Government--the three branches (judicial, legislative, executive.

Presidents.

Language Arts: Root words--learn to identify what a word means by using prefixes, suffixes, and root words.

Parts of speech--noun, verbs, adjectives, adverbs, proper nouns, pronouns, conjunctions, articles.

Fiction.

Nonfiction.

What is the author's purpose for writing, and what is the main idea of the story?

Learn how to write a paragraph (topic sentence, supporting details, conclusion).

Learn about transitional words and phrases.

Punctuation.

<u>Math</u>: Addition and subtraction up to four digit numbers (4532+3614=).

Multiplication tables.

Division problems.

Graphs.

Polygons.

Lines.

Solids--cubes, cones, cylinders.

Money--making change.

Word problems.

BOOKS FOR YOUR THIRD GRADER

"How to Make an Apple Pie and See the World" by Marjorie Priceman.

"Fairy Tale Feasts" by Jane Yolen and Heidi E. Stemple (a cookbook).

"I and You and Don't Forget Who" by Brian Cleary (a book about prepositions) one in a series.

"Mapping Penny's World" by Loreen Leedy.

"Are We There Yet?" by Alison Lester (a book about Australia).

"Because of Winn Dixie" by Kate Dicamillo.

"The Conquerors" by David McKee.

"Dare to Dream Series" by Carl Sommert.

"Anelia to Zora: 26 Women Who Changed the World" by Cynthia Chin-lee.

"Author: A True Story by Helen Lester (inspire your child to write).

"Clean Sea: Story of Rachel Carson" by Carol Hilgartner.

"Leonardo da Vinci" by Diane Stanley.

"So You Want to Be an Explorer" by Judith St. George (one in a series).

"The Very First Americans (Reading Railroad)" by John Herman.

"What if You Met a Pirate" by Jan Adkins.

"Ultimate Chess" by Jon Tremaine.

"The Greg Tang Math Series."

"Sir Cumference and the Dragon of Pi" by Cindy Neuschwander.

"Math Curse" by Jon Scieszka.

"Arithmetricks" by Edward H. Julius.

"What's Your Angle, Pythagoras? A Math Adventure" by Julie Ellis.

"Secrets of Mental Math: The Mathemagicians Guide to Lightning Calculation and Amazing Math Tricks" by Arthur Benjamin and Michael Shermer.

"Ray's Arithmetic Series" by Joseph Ray. (Written in the 1870's, this series teaches children math in a way that they can apply it in real life situations.)

"Ben and Me" by Robert Lawson (a book about Ben Franklin told by a mouse).

"A Child's History of the World" by V.M. Hillyer.

"What Your Third Grader Needs to Know" by E.D. Hirsch.

"Escape From Mr. Lemoncello's Library" by Chris Grabensteion (fun, clue-solving mystery).

"Magic Tree House Series, and Magic Tree House Fact Trackers" by Mary Pope Osborne and Natalie Pope Boyce (fun history reads).

"Schoolhouse Rock (Special 30th Anniversary Edition) (2010)" by Jack Sheldon, Darrell Stern, and Tom Warburton (DVD) Great videos and songs on all sorts of subjects. Check these out; your kids will love them.

"Meet the Orchestra" by Ann Hayes and Karmen Thompson.

"Latitude and Longitude (Rookie Read About Geography)" by Rebecca Aberg.

"Read and Understand Science" by Evan Moor Educational Publishers.

"Liberty Lee's Tail of Independence" by Cheryl Shaw Barnes and Peter W. Barnes (one in a series from Little Patriot Press). The series is great for studying our government and country: House Mouse, Senate Mouse, Woodrow for President, Woodrow the White House Mouse.

"The Story of the Star Spangled Banner" by Patricia A. Pingry and Nancy Munger.

"Red, White, and Blue (Penguin Young Readers, L3)" by John Herman.

"National Geographic Kids Big Book of Space" by Catherine D. Hughes and David A. Aguilar.

"National Geographic Readers: Planets" by Elizabeth Carney.

"Forces Make Things Move (Let's-Read-and-Find-Out 2)" by Kimberly Brubaker Bradley and Paul Meisel.

"How Do You Lift a Lion?" by Robert E. Wells.

"The Magic School Bus Jumping into Electricity" by the Magic School Bus.

"Charged Up: The Story of Electricity (Science Works)" by Jacqui Bailey and Matthew Lilly.

"A is for Abigail: An Almanac of Amazing American Women" by Lynne Cheney and Robin Preiss Glasser.

"Yucky Worms: Read and Wonder" by Vivian French and Jessice Ahlberg.

"What Do Roots Do?" by Kathleen V. Kudlinski.

"An Earthworm's Life (Nature Upclose)" by John Himmelman.

"Gardening Wizardy for Kids" by L. Patricia Kite.

"Secrets of the Garden: Food Chains and the Food Web in Our Backyard" by Kathleen Weidner Zoehfeld and Priscilla Lamont.

"The Wright Brothers: Pioneers of American Aviation (Landmark Books)" by Quentin Reynolds.

"Seaman's Journal: On the Trail With Lewis and Clark" by Patti Reeder Eubank.

"Lewis and Clark and Me: A Dog's Tale" by Laurie Myers and Michael Dooling.

"The Life and Times of the Ant" by Charles Micucci.

Trail of Tears (Step-Into-Reading, Step 5) by Joseph Bruchac.

"Westward Expansion" (An Interactive--You Choose Books--One in a Series: The California Gold Rush, The Underground Railroad etc.)

"On a Beam of Light: A Story of Albert Einstein" by Jeffifer Berne and Vladimir Radunsky.

"The Boy who Loved Math, The Improbable Life of Paul Erdos" by Deborah Heiligman and LeUyen Pham.

"Bedtime Math" by Laura Overdeck and Jim Paillot.

"Your Fantastic Elastic Brain" by JoAnn Deak Ph.D and Sarah Ackerley.

"Roots, Shoots, Buckets, and Boots: Gardening Together with Children" by Sharon LoveJoy.

WHAT MY CHILD NEEDS TO KNOW FOR FOURTH GRADE

<u>Science</u>: Classify plants and animal, characteristics inherited or learned.

Environments--different organisms that live in each environment and how they adapt to their surroundings.

Sun and the Moon--production of light and how the Moon reflects the light from the Sun; the Moon's phases.

Constellations.

Position of the Earth and the planets.

Clouds--different types and how they are formed.

Magnetism.

Static electricity.

Circuits.

Conductors.

Characteristics of light.

Social Studies: Hemispheres.

Regions of U.S.--Northeast, Southwest, Midwest, West, South.

Research resources--books, newspapers, photographs, internet, speeches, and letters.

Current events.

Know the fifty states and their capitols, state and national symbols; president, vice president, and state governor.

History: World history.

American history.

Government--state and federal, "Articles of Confederation," Representatives and Senators, and "The System of Checks and Balances."

The Constitutional Convention.

Language Arts: Cursive writing.

Homophones.

Writing process--prewriting, drafting, revising, editing, publishing.

Write a five-paragraph paper.

Styles of writing--expository, descriptive, persuasive, narrative.

Prepositions.

Punctuation.

Math: Length, weight, capacity, and temperature.

Metric system.

Mode, medium, mean.

Rounding numbers.

Decimals.

Fractions--multiplying, dividing.

Add and subtract fractions with same denominator.

Convert fractions to decimals and decimals to fractions.

Learn to use a calculator.

Graphs--bar, circle, line.

Place value to the millions.

Number line.

Algebra--order of operations.

Parentheses--5x4 is the same thing as 5(4).

Geometry--points, lines, rays, right angles, obtuse angles, acute angles, perpendicular lines, parallel lines, intersecting lines.

Draw and recognize polygons up to eight sides.

Congruent means the same thing as equal to. Learn how to tell if a polygon is congruent.

BOOKS FOR YOUR FOURTH GRADER

"The Misadventures of Maude March" by Audry Couloumbis.

"Pirateology" by Dugald A. Steer (one in a series).

"Beezus and Ramona" by Beverly Cleary.

"Math Curse" by Jon Scieszka.

"The Shakespeare Stealer" by Gary Blackwood.

"The Best of Times: Math Stratagies That Multiply" by Gregory Tang.

"Top Secret: A Handbook of Codes, Ciphers, and Secret Writing."

"Speed Math for Kids: The Fast and Fun Way to Do Basic Calculations" by Bill Handley.

"What Your Fourth Grader Needs to Know" by E. D. Hirsh.

"Leonardo da Vinci" by Diane Stanley (one in a series).

"The American Story: 100 True Tales From American History" by Jennifer Armstrong.

"Magic Tree House Series, Magic Tree House Fact Trackers" by Mary Pope Osborne and Natalie Pope Boyce (fun history read).

"From Sea to Shining Sea for Young Readers: 1787-1837 (Discovering God's

Plan For America)" by Peter Marshall, David Manuel, and Anna Wilson Fishel.

"Light and the Glory for Young Readers: 1492-1787 (Discovering God's Plan for America)."

"Sounding Forth the Trumpet for Young Readers: 1837-1860 (Discovering God's Plan for America)."

"George vs George: The American Revolution as Seen from Both Sides" by Rosalyn Schanzer.

"Jean Fritz History Book Series: What's the Big Idea, Ben Franklin? Will You Sign Here, John Hancock? And Then What Happened Paul Revere? Can't You Make Them Behave, King George? Shh! We're Writing the Constitution. Why Don't You

Get a Horse, Sam Adams? Where Was Patrick Henry on the 29th of May? Where Do You Think You're Going Christopher Columbus?"

"Escape From Mr. Lemoncello's Library" by Chris Grabenstein (fun read; clue solving mystery).

"The Indian in the Cupboard Series" by Lynne Reid Banks (fun read).

"The Wright Brothers: Pioneers of American Aviation" (Landmark Books) by Quentin Reynold.

"Brown Paper School Book: Blood and Guts" by Linda Allison (a book about the body with experiments).

"Lewis and Clark and Me: A Dog's Tale" by Laurie Myers and Michael Dooling.

"Basher Basics: Weather: Whipping Up a Storm" by Simon Basher and Dan Green.

"Fizz, Bubble and Flash: Element Explorations and Atom Adventures for Hands-on Science Fun!" (Williamson Kids Can Series) by Ph.D Brandolini Anita and Michael P. Kline.

"The Diary of Remember Patience Whipple" by Kathryn Lasky.

"Timeless Thomas: How Thomas Edison Changed Our Lives" by Gene Barretta.

"Now and Ben: The Modern Inventions of Benjamin Franklin" by Gene Barretta.

"Neo Leo: The Ageless Idea of Leonardo da Vinci" by Gene Barretta.

"Mistakes That Worked" by Charlotte Jones and John Obrien (Forty Familiar Inventions and How They Came to Be).

"Trail of Tears (Step-Into-Reading, Step 5)" by Joseph Bruchac.

"Westward Expansion: An Interactive History Adventure" by Allison Lassieur (You Choose Books) One in a series:

    The California Gold Rush

    The Underground Railroad

    The Wild West

    Colonial America

    The Civil War

    The Revolutionary War

    Exploring the New World

The Great Depression

WWI

WWII

The Alamo

Ancient Egypt

The Dust Bowl

The Attack on Pearl Harbor

"A Child's Introduction to the Night Sky: The Story of the Stars, Planets, and Constellations--and How You Can Find Them in the Sky" by Michael Driscoll and Meredith Hamilton.

"The Who Was Series"

Neil Armstrong

Albert Einstein

Thomas Alva Edison

Walt Disney

Amelia Earhart

Abraham Lincoln

Steve Jobs

Amedeus Mozart

Leonardo da Vinci

Martin Luther King, Jr.

Ben Franklin

"On a Beam of Light: A Story of Albert Einstein" by Jennifer Berne and Vladimir Radunsky.

"The Boy Who Loved Math: The Improbable Life of Paul Erdos" by Deborah Heiligman and Leuyen Pham.

"Math Matters Series."

"What Was the Gold Rush? by Joan Holub and Tim Tomkinson. "What Was" Series:

    Boston Tea Party

    Battle of Gettysburg

    March on Washington

    Pearl Harbor

    The Alamo

"The First Thanksgiving" by Joan Holub.

"Our Constitution Rocks" by Juliette Turner.

"What Would the Founding Fathers Think: Young American's Guide to Understanding What Makes Our Nation Great and How We've Strayed" by David Bownan.

"Roots, Shoots, Buckets, and Boots: Gardening Together with Children" by Sharon Lovejoy.

"An Earthworm's Life (Nature Up Close)" by John Himmelman.

"Gardening Wizardy for Kids" by L. Patricia Kite.

"Amazing Biome Projects You Can Build Yourself (Build it Yourself Series)" by Donna Latham and Farah Rizvi.

"Tell Me, Tree: All About Trees for Kids" by Gail Gibbons.

"Explore Rocks and Minerals: Great Projects, Activities, Experiments (Explore

Your World Series)" by Cynthia Light Brown, Nick Brown, and Bryan Stone.

"Why Spacemen Can't Burp" by Mitchell Symons.

"Smart About the Presidents (Smart About History Series)" by Jon Buller, Maryann Cocca Lefflerm, Dana Regan, Susan Saunders, and Jill Weber.

"50 States: A State-by-State Tour of the USA" by Erin Mchugh and Albert Schrier.

"Explore Life Cycles: 25 Great Projects, Activities, Experiments (Explore Your World Series)" by Kathleen M. Reilly and Bryan Stone.

"Secrets of the Garden: Food Chains and the Food Web in Our Backyard" by

Kathleen Weidner Zoehfeld and Priscilla Lamont.

WHAT MY CHILD NEEDS TO KNOW
FOR FIFTH GRADE

<u>Science</u>: Organs, cells, how systems of the body work together.

Ecosystems.

Food web.

Producers.

Decomposers.

Consumers.

Predators.

Prey.

Five major kingdoms--plants, fungi, protists, monerans.

Water cycle--evaporation, precipitation, condensation.

Earth layers.

Rocks and fossils.

States of matter.

Periodic table.

Force.

Why do we have waves?

History: American History--Native Americans, early explorers, 13 original colonies, American Revolution, Civil War.

<u>Social Studies</u>: Current events, knowledge of basic copyright laws, meanings and consequences of plagiarism, cyber security do's and don'ts.

Map scale.

Climate zones.

Time zones.

<u>Computer</u>: Researching and writing an essay, cutting, pasting, spell check, typing, power point presentation, photo editing skills; use program to organize data and create graphs.

<u>Language Arts</u>: Direct objects, indirect objects.

Agreement in number and gender.

Nominative and objective case.

Imagery, metaphor, symbolism.

Do a book report.

Keep a journal.

Know how to write a five-paragraph paper using the writing process.

Have correct punctuation, capitalization, and sentence structure when writing.

Learn how to make an outline.

Know what these are and how to use them--index, glossary, title page, introduction, preface, appendix.

Math:

Use math in real life situations.

Place value, addition, subtraction, multiplying, dividing, word problems.

Negative and positive.

Pre-algebra-solve equations with an unknown variable ($5y+2=12$).

Fractions, percentages, and decimals.

GCF or Greatest Common Factor.

Equivalent.

Lowest terms.

Mixed numbers.

Geometry--points, line segments, rays, planes.

Triangles--equilateral, right, scalene, isosceles.

Measuring angles.

Formulas:

Area of a polygon a=lw; volume of a prism v=lwh; area of a parallelogram a=b x h; pi=3.14.

Diameter of a circle (the length from one side of a circle to the other side of a circle).

Radius of a circle (radius is half the diameter).

Circumference, or distance around it, of a circle c=pi x d; circumference equals pi times diameter.

Perimeter of a rectangle P=2-(l+w); perimeter equals 2 x length plus width.

Perimeter of a square P=4s, 4 times side.

Perimeter of a triangle =p=s+s+s; perimeter equals side plus side plus side.

Perimeter of a parallelogram P=2 (b+s); perimeter equals 2 times base plus side.

Use a protractor.

Use a compass.

Ratios.

Averages.

Graphs.

BOOKS FOR YOUR FIFTH GRADER

"The Phantom Tollbooth" by Norton Juster.

"The Secret Garden" by Frances Burnett.

"The Mystery of Rascal Pratt" by Robbie Scott and Gary Cianciarula.

"Encyclopedia Brown Cracks the Case" by Donald J. Sobol (uses science and history to solve mysteries).

"Pollyanna" by Eleanor Porter.

"Emeril's, There's a Chef in My World! Recipes that Take You Places," by Emeril Lagasse.

"Arithmetricks: 50 Easy Ways to Add and Subtract, Multiply and Divide" by Edward H. Julius.

"What Your Fifth Grader Needs to Know" by E.D. Hirsch.

"The American Revolution for Kids: A History With 21 Activities" (one in a series).

"Christopher Columbus' First Voyage to America From the Log of the *Santa Maria*" by Christopher Columbus.

"Speed Math for Kids: The Fast and Fun Way to Do Basic Calculations" by Bill Handley.

"The Indian in the Cupboard Series" by Lynne Reid Banks (fun read).

"Escape From Mr. Lemoncello's Library" by Chris Grabenstein (fun read, clue-solving mystery).

"The Children's Homer: The Adventures of Odysseus and the Tale of Troy" by Padraic Colum (Greek Mythology).

"What was the Gold Rush?" by Joan Holub and Tim Tomkinson (What Was Series):

  Boston Tea Party

  Battle of Gettysburg

  March on Washington

  Pearl Harbor

  The Alamo

"The First Thanksgiving" by Joan Holub.

"Our Constitution Rocks" by Juliette Turner.

"A Child's Introduction to the Night Sky: The Story of the Stars, Planets, and Constellations--and How You Can Find Them in the Sky" by Michael Driscoll and Meredith Hamilton.

"Who Was Series"
    Neil Armstrong
    Albert Einstein
    Thomas Alva Edison
    Walt Disney
    Amelia Earhart
    Dr. Seuss
    Abraham Lincoln

Steve Jobs

Amedeus Mosart

Leonardo da Vinci

Martin Luther King, Jr.

Ben Franklin

"Roots, Shoots, Buckets, and Boots: Gardening Together with Children" by Sharon Lovejoy.

"Gardening Wizardy for Kids (Nature Up Close)" by John Himmelman.

"Life Science, Grades 5-8 (The 100+ Series)."

"Amazing Biome Projects You Can Build Yourself (Build it Yourself Series)" by Donna Latham and Farah Rizvi.

"Get Real: What kind of World are You Buying?" by Mara Rockliff.

"Why Spacemen Can't Burp" by Mitchell Symons.

"Smart About the Presidents (Smart About History)" by Jon Buller, Maryann Cocca Leffler, Dana Regan, Susan Saunders, and Jill Weber.

"50 States: A State-by-State Tour of the USA" by Erin McHugh and Albert Schrier.

"The Diary of Remember Patience Whipple" by Kathryn Lasky.

"Timeless Thomas: How Thomas Edison Changed Our Lives" by Gene Barretta (One in a Series).

"Now and Ben: The Modern Inventions of Benjamin Franklin."

"Neo Leo: The Ageless Idea of Leonardo da Vinci."

"Mistakes That Worked" by Charlotte Jones and John Obrien (40 Familiar Inventions and How They Came to Be).

"Westward Expansion: An Interactive History Adventure" by Allison Lassieur (You Choose Books) One in a Series:

    The California Gold Rush

    The Underground Railroad

    The Wild West

    Colonial America

    The Civil War

    The Revolutionary War

    The Great Depression

WWI

WWII

The Alamo

Ancient Egypt

The Dust Bowl

The Attack on Pearl Harbor

"The Wright Brothers: Pioneers of American Aviation" (Landmark Books) By Quentin Reynolds.

"Brown Paper School Book: Blood and Guts" by Linda Allison (a book about the body with experiments).

"Lewis and Clark and Me: A Dog's Tale" by Laurie Myers and Michael Dooling.

"Basher Basics: Weather--Whipping Up a Storm" by Simon Basher and Dan Green.

"The Mystery of the Periodic Table" (Living History Library) by Benjamin D. Wiker, Jeanne Bendick, and Theodore Schluenderfritz.

"Fizz, Bubble, and Flash: Element Explorations and Atom Adventures for Hands-On Science Fun! (Williamson Kids Can Series)" by Ph.D Brandolini Anita and Michael P. Kline.

"Liberty's Kids: Books and/or DVDs."

"Knights and Castles (Magic Tree House Research Guide)" by Mary Osborne, Will Osborne, and Sal Murdocca.

"The Horrible, Miserable, Middle Ages: The Disgusting Details About Life During Medieval Times (Disgusting History)" by Kathy Allen.

"The Minstrel in the Tower" (Stepping Stone) by Gloria Skurzynski.

WHAT MY CHILD NEEDS TO KNOW
FOR SIXTH GRADE

<u>Science</u>: Cells--plant and animal.

Reproduction.

Biomes.

Muscular system.

Organ system.

Skeletal system.

Weather.

Earth's atmosphere.

Atoms.

Molecules.

Elements.

Periodic table.

Volume.

Density.

Solubility.

Compounds.

Mixtures.

Acids.

Bases.

<u>Social Studies</u>: Ancient Civilizations.

<u>American History</u>: WWI, WWII, Korea.

<u>Language Arts</u>: Personal narrative, descriptive writing, explanatory exposition, persuasive, and business letter writing.

First person.

Latin roots, prefixes, suffixes.

Fact and opinion.

Different kinds of poems.

Composition writing.

Thesis statement.

Transitional words and phrases.

Conclusion.

Pronouns and proper case (subjective, objective, possessive).

Pronoun--number and person.

<u>Math</u>: Pre-algebra.

Multiply and divide fractions, mixed numbers, and decimals.

Percentages.

Statistics and probability.

Order of operations.

Metric units.

Graphs and tables.

Word problems.

Area of a circle.

Area of a triangle.

Circumference.

Parallelograms.

Ratios and proportions.

Greatest common factor.

Least common multiple.

Volume=lxwxh.

Volume=bxh.

How to use a calculator.

BOOKS FOR YOUR SIXTH GRADER

"The Amazing Expedition Bible" by Mary Hollingsworth (world history tied together with the Bible).

"The World Almanac for Kids."

"Beautiful Stories From Shakespeare for Children" by E. Nesbit.

"The Declaration of Independence" by Elaine Londau.

"Ray's Arithmetic" by Joseph Ray.

"What Your Sixth Grader Needs to Know" by E.D. Hirsch.

"The Boy in the Striped Pajamas" by John Boyne (Holocaust).

"Number the Stars" by Lois Lowry.

"The Diary of Anne Frank" by Anne Frank.

"Baseball in April and Other Stories" by Gary Soto (short stories).

"Hatchet" by Gary Paulsen (action adventure survival story).

"The True Confessions of Charlotte Doyle" by Avi.

"Weedflower" by Cynthia Kadohata (Japanese Internment Camps).

"The Wright Brothers, Pioneers of American Aviation" (Landmark Books) by Quentin Reynolds.

"Brown Paper School Book: Blood and Guts" by Linda Allison (a book about the body with experiments).

"Lewis and Clark and Me: A Dog's Tale" by Laurie Myers and Michael Dooling.

"Basher Science: Algebra and Geometry" by Dan Green and Simon Basher.

"The Mystery of the Periodic Table" (Living History Library) by Benjamin D. Wiker, Jeanne Bendick, and Theodore Schluenderfritz.

"Fizz, Bubble, and Flash: Element Explorations and Atom Adventures for Hands-On-Science Fun!" (Williamson Kids Can Series) by Ph.D Brandolini Anita and Michael P. Kline.

"The Diary of Remember Patience Whipple" by Kathryn Lasky.

"Mistakes That Worked" by Charlotte Jones and John Obrien (40 Familiar Inventions and How They Came to Be).

"Uncle John's Bathroom Reader for Kids Only" by Bathroom Readers Institute.

"Smart About the Presidents (Smart About History)" by Jon Buller, Maryann Cocca Leffler, Dana Regan, Susan Saunders, and Jill Weber.

"Gardening Wizardy for Kids" by L. Patricia Kite.

"Life Science, Grades 5-8" (The 100+ Series).

"Amazing Biome Projects You Can Build Yourself (Build it Yourself Series)" by Donna Latham and Farah Rizvi.

"A Child's Introduction to the Night Sky: The Story of the Stars, Planets, and Constellations--and How You Can Find Them in the Sky" by Michael Driscoll and Meredith Hamilton.

"Who Was Series"

    Neil Armstrong

    Albert Einstein

    Thomas Alva Edison

    Walt Disney

    Amelia Earhart

    Abraham Lincoln

    Steve Jobs

    Amedeus Mozart

Leonardo da Vinci

Martin Luther King, Jr.

Ben Franklin

"What Was the Gold Rush?" by Joan Holub and Tim Tomkinson.

"What Was Series"

Boston Tea Party

Battle of Gettysburg

March on Washington

Pearl Harbor

The Alamo

"The First Thanksgiving" by Joan Holub.

"Our Constitution Rocks" by Juliette Turner.

"What Would the Founding Fathers Think: A Young American's Guide to Understanding What Makes Our Nation Great and How We've Strayed" by David Bownan.

"Code Talker: A Novel About the Navajo Marines of World War II" by Joseph Bruchac.

HOMESCHOOLING YOUR HIGHSCHOOLER

My main goal in homeschooling is to teach my children how to be self-taught and self-motivated. By the time my children were in high school, I could provide them with their educational resources, and they could plan their course of study. Now I know you are thinking, "Wow, if I did that, my teen wouldn't do anything?"

I'm not saying that was the end of my involvement. Teens will be teens, and you definitely need to keep an eye on their progress and give them quite a few nudges and, in some cases, forceful pushes in the right direction. I have found, though, that if you pick subjects in which they are even halfway interested, you don't have to push too hard. If your teen has any clue as to what he/she wants to do for a career, let them study subjects that relate to that, if possible.

Of course there are requirements they have to fulfill to graduate. You will need to check with your State or cover group to see what those are. When you find out, be creative in how you fulfill them.

For instance, if you need three credits in history, one credit equals 175 days of study in a certain subject. Don't simply throw a history book at them but instead allow them to learn history through a variety of fiction and nonfiction books that they can really sink their teeth into. Also, go on historical field trips. History is just waiting to be discovered around every corner, so take advantage of these opportunities.

I like to use unconventional books like "Passing the New (your State) Graduation

Examination." These books are a "Reader's Digest" version of everything they should know when they graduate. There are several books that cover various subjects such as social studies, science, etc; and they are presented in workbook form. You can follow along with the book or, if something is really interesting, you can research the subject further on your own.

I also like study books for passing the General Education Diploma (GED). It's like the other books but covers all subjects under one cover. These books are great for pinpointing subjects in which you need extra help. Then there are the ACT and SAT study guides. It's never too early to start practicing for these tests.

Another good idea for your high school student is to get him or her involved in co-op or extra classes that your cover group might offer. My first cover group had a program called LIFT that was for ninth grade and up. The group met once a week, and each student could take up to four classes for a certain amount of money per class. I have had a new group for the last two years, and we have a co-op. It works the same way, but the classes are free.

These classes are great for teens because they get to socialize with other homeschool families, and it also gives them an incentive to do their school work and do it right because they want to do well in front of their peers.

There are dual enrollment classes that your teen can take at some local colleges. These classes count as high school credits and college credits at the same time. The classes give your teen a head start on their first year of college while completing their high school classes. Be careful, though; schools are now notorious for not transferring credits from one college to another.

If this turns out to be the case, your teen will have to take the class twice, which could be quite boring. To find out about dual enrollment, call your local colleges and check with the college your child is planning on attending after graduation to see if their classes will transfer.

Another great way to keep your teen focused and ready for college is volunteer work. My boys volunteered for Habitat for Humanity. Not only did they enjoy getting out and meeting new people, they learned a tremendous amount about building houses, and it's great for college transcripts. It was a win-win situation, and the leaders of Habitat loved having their help.

My kids also get involved in a Christmas charity every year. This is such an eye opener for them and such a blessing at the same time.

One of the most important things for your teen is to keep them involved with other teenagers. Our support group had wonderful parents who were highly involved with their teen, and together we planned and executed great events for our children.

We had boys' club for the teen boys. They met once a month and did outdoor activities. They hiked, camped, played paint ball, and other types of sports. Sometimes they just liked to hang out.

Our teen girls had a similar club, and they did things teenage girls liked to do.

The girls actually planned their own calendar.

We had "lunch bunch" twice a month where the boys and girls would get together at someone's home. They brought their lunch, ate, and socialized for the afternoon.

We had teens' day out where we planned an event once a month such as putt-putt, hayrides, picnicking, scavenger hunts, movie nights, day trips, campouts, dances, etc.

We had a photography club where we went to different sites and did photo shoots, then their work was showcased on their club website.

But let me stress to you that none of these things are possible without strong parental involvement. This may sound like a lot of work for the parents, but trust me; you are going to blink and your teen will be grown and gone. Take this time to get involved in his or her life and share a bond that the two of you will never forget. Not only will you have a happy, fulfilled teen, but you will have a great relationship and wonderful memories with your child that will last a lifetime.

Last but not least, make sure you indulge your teen's interests. If they like sports, find them a sports team to join. There are city leagues, gymnastic centers, cover group sports teams, church teams, and YMCA teams. You may have to search for them, but they are out there.

My sons and one of my daughters played soccer all through high school. My oldest son even received a college scholarship because of soccer. My daughters took gymnastics, and my oldest daughter taught classes after she graduated.

If your teen likes cars, get them an old clunker and let them work on it. My boys can take apart a whole car and put it back together. They never took an automotive class; they figured it out themselves by using the automotive manuals and trial and error tactics.

If they like to act, find a theatrical group for them to join. My youngest daughter was in a play with The Way Off Broadway Players, a theatrical group in our town, and she had a blast. She also took acting classes one summer at a local college and got to showcase her acting skills there.

If they like to cook, let them take a cooking class or let them cook special meals at home for the family. Give them recipes from different countries to try out.

If you have an entrepreneur on your hands, give them the tools to start their own business, such as a lawn service. Let them see the pros and cons of working so they will understand what real life is all about. This may even help them find the direction that will eventually fulfill their careers.

If they like to build things, give them the tools to get started. My boys and their friends would find construction sites and ask if they could have the scrap wood. The builders were more than happy to give it to them. They built all kinds of forts and even built their own paint ball course. One of the boys sold bird houses, and my youngest son built a farm house table for my kitchen that will seat ten people.

There is also the Civil Air Patrol (CAP) that recruits teenagers. This organization teaches them how to work as a team. They can actually learn to fly and how to do search and rescue work. They then put their skills to work with real rescue missions.

Just remember, this is a time of discovery and enlightenment for teens, and you need to keep their minds wholesome and their hands busy. With a little—no, I mean a lot of—support and help from you, this can be a wonderful time in your child's life, a time both of you can enjoy.

BOOKS FOR YOUR HIGHSCHOOLER

"Seven Miracles That Saved America" by Chris and Ted Stewart.

"Seven Tipping Points That Saved the World" by Chris and Ted Stewart.

"A Patriot's History of the United States" by Larry Schweikart and Michael Allen.

"The Five Thousand Year Leap" by W. Cleon Skousen.

"The Real George Washington" by Jay A. Parry.

"The Real Thomas Jefferson" by Jay A. Parry.

"The Real Ben Franklin" by Jay A. Parry.

"Being George Washington," Glenn Beck.

"The Jungle" by Upton Sinclair.

"War Letters: Extraordinary Correspondence from American Wars" by Andrew Carroll.

"The Yanks are Coming" by Albert Marrin.

"Sargent York and the Great War: His Own Life Story and War Diary."

"A History of US: War, Peace, and All That Jazz" by Joy Hakim.

"The Great Gatsby" by F. Scott Fitzgerald.

"The Grapes of Wrath" by John Steinbeck.

"To Kill a Mockingbird" by Harper Lee.

"The Glass Menagerie" by Tennessee Williams.

"Desert Exile" by Yashiko Uchida.

"Americans Remember the Home Front" by Roy Hoopes.

"Torpedo Junction" by Homer Hickam.

"The Hiding Place" by Corrie Ten Boom.

"A History of US: All the People" by Joy Hakim.

"Remembering Jim Crow: African Americans Tell About Life in the Segregated South" by William Chafe.

"Animal Farm" by George Orwell.

"The Martyred" by Richard Kim.

"America and Vietnam" by Albert Marrin.

"The Everlasting Hatred" by Hal Lindsey.

"The Old Man and the Sea" by Ernest Hemingway.

"The Seafarer" (Author Unknown).

"Beowulf" (Author Unknown).

"The Ecclesiastical History of the English People" by Venerable Bede.

"The Canterbury Tales" by Geoffrey Chaucer.

"Sir Gawain and The Green Knight" (Author Unknown).

"Shakespeare's Sonnets."

"King John" by William Shakespeare.

"Paradise Lost" by John Milton.

"Gulliver's Travels" by Jonathan Swift.

"David Copperfield" by Charles Dickens.

"Pride and Prejudice" by Jane Austen.

"Dr. Jekyll and Mr. Hyde" by Robert Louis Stevenson.

"Killing Lincoln: The Shocking Assassination that Changed America Forever" by Bill O'Reilly and Martin Dugard.

"Killing Kennedy: The End of Camelot" by Bill O'Reilly and Martin Dugard.

"Killing Patton: The Strange Death of World War II's Most Audacious General" by Bill O'Reilly and Martin Dugard.

"Lincoln's Last Days: The Shocking Assassination That Changed America Forever" by Bill O'Reilly and Dwight Jon Zimmerman (ages 10-18).

"Kennedy's Last Days: The Assassination That Defined a Generation" by Bill O'Reilly (ages 10-18).

"Rush Revere and the Brave Pilgrims: Time-Travel Adventures with Exceptional Americans" by Rush Limbaugh.

"Rush Revere and the First Patriots: Time-Travel Adventures With Exceptional Americans" by Rush Limbaugh.

"What is Relativity? An Intuitive Introduction to Einstein's Ideas and Why They Matter" by Jeffrey Bennett.

"Code Talker: A Novel About the Navajo Marines of World War II" by Joseph Bruchac.

"Study Guides for Your State's Graduation Examination and GED Study Guides." (These books are helpful in letting you know what your teen should be learning, then you can let them delve further into the subjects in which they are interested.)

Look Up Online: "Travels Through Time: Nonfiction History Books for Teens" by Keith Barlog. (This is a great list of books that will keep the love of reading and learning embedded in your teens.)

Part of this list was generously given to us by Lee Gonet, one of the greatest history teachers of all times. Thanks, Lee!!

TEACHER'S HELPERS
(Cheat Sheets)

METRIC SYSTEM

<u>Mass</u>: Measures the matter in an object. It is the same everywhere.

<u>Weight</u>: How hard a planet's gravity pulls on an object. You would weigh one amount at home, a different amount on a high mountain, and something totally different on the Moon.

<u>Newton</u>: Measures weight.

<u>Gram</u>: Measures mass.

<u>Meter</u>: Measures distance.

<u>Liter</u>: Measures volume.

<u>Second</u>: Measures time.

METRIC PREFIXES

Milli—one thousandth 0.001.

Centi—one hundredth 0.01.

Kilo—one thousand 1000.

Milligram—1/1000 of a gram.

Millimeter—1/1000 of a meter.

Milliliter—1/1000 of a liter.

Centigram—1/100 of a gram.

Centimeter—1/100 of a gram.

Centiliter—1/100 of a liter.

Kilogram—1000 grams.

Kilometer—1000 meters.

Kiloliter—1000 liters.

Gram—the mass of a housefly.

Meter—the length from your right shoulder to the tip of your left hand fingers.

Liter—Think of a two-liter drink bottle; four liters is one gallon.

http//www.dummies.com//how-to/ content/how-to-use-the-metric-system.html

TOP TEN IMPORTANT EVENTS IN U.S. HISTORY

10. Assassination of Abraham Lincoln.

9. Louisiana Purchase. Thomas Jefferson double the size of America when he purchased the land from France.

8. Manhattan Project; the creation of the atomic bomb.

7. Vietnam War.

6. Death of Osama bin Laden.

5. Assassination of John F. Kennedy.

4. The American Revolution.

3. The Civil War.

2. September 11, 2001; terrorists fly planes into Twin Towers in New York City.

1. Apollo II.

www.listverse.com/2011/07/14/top-10-important-events-in-us-history/

U.S. HISTORY

Colonial Life (1607-1760s).

Prologue to Revolution and Revolutionary War (1754-1783).

Articles of Confederation Period and Federalist Era (1781-1800).

Jeffersonian Era and War of 1812 (1801-1819.

Nathanalism and Sectionalism (1800-1850).

Jacksonian Era (1828-1840s) and Reform Movements in the 19th Century (1800-1850).

Immigration and Expansionism (1820-1850s).

Antebellum Period and Civil War (1850-1865).

Reconstruction and Gilded Age (1865-1900).

Progressive Era and World War I (1900-1919).

Great Depression (1920-1939).

World War II (1939-1945).

1960s (1960-1969).

Contemporary America (1970-present).

"U.S. History Resources," Greg D. Feldmeth.

SYSTEMS OF THE HUMAN BODY

The circulatory system

The digestive system.

The endocrine system.

The excretory system.

The immune and lymph systems.

The muscular system.

The nervous system.

The reproductive system.

The respiratory system.

The sensory system.

The skeletal system.

PREPOSITIONS

Aboard	Below
About	Beneath
Above	Beside
Across	Between
After	Beyond
Against	But
Along	By
Amid	Concerning
Among	Considering
Anti	Despite
Around	Down
As	During
At	Except
Atop	Excluding
Before	Following
Behind	For

From	Over
Given	Past
In	Per
Including	Plus
Inside	Regarding
Into	Round
Like	Save
Minus	Since
Near	Than
Next	Through
Of	Throughout
Off	To
On	Toward
Onto	Under
Opposite	Underneath
Out	Unlike
Outside	Until

Unto	Via
Up	With
Upon	Within
Versus	Worth

www.englishclub.com/grammer/prepo-sitionslist.htm

GREEK AND LATIN ROOT WORDS

Ad	to, toward
Am, amor	liking, love
Anti	old, against
Aqua	water
Arbor	tree
Arts, artis	art, skill
Aster, astr	star
Aud, aus	hear, listen
Autos	self
Belli	war
Biblos	book
Bios	life
Bonus	good
Brev	short
Cad, cas	to fall
Capit, capt	head

Centum	hundred
Chronos	time
Clam, claim	cry out
Cognoac, gnosi	know
Corpus, Corporis	body
Cred	believe
Cresc, crease, Cru	rise, grow
Dem	people
Dent, don't	tooth
Derm	skin
Dict	say, speak
Discipulus	student
Doc	teach
Domin	master
Don	give
Dormio, dormitum	sleep
Duo	two

Dura	hard, long lasting
Dynam	power
Fall, fals	deceive
Flex, flect	bend
Fort, forc	strong
Fract, frag	break
Frater, fratris	brother
Gam	marriage
Geo	earth
Graph	write
Grat	pleasing
Helio	Sunday
Hema, hemo	blood
Hetero	different
Homo	same
Hydros	water
Hypnos	sleep

Ignis	fire
Inter	between
Lau, lav, lot, lut	wash
Leg	law
Liber	free
Logos	word
Luc, lum, lus, lun	light
Luna	moon
Magn	great
Magnus	large
Man	hand, by hand
Mand	command
Mania	madness
Mar, mari, mer	sea, pool
Matri	mother
Mega	great
Mem	remember

Micro	small
Migra	wander
Mille	thousand
Multi	many, much
Nov	new
Novem	nine
Octo	eight
Oper	work
Ortho	straight, correct
Pac	peace
Pater, part	father
Path, pathy	feeling, suffering
Ped, pod	foot
Pedo	child
Phobos	fear
Phon	sound
Photos	light

Pop	people
Port	carry
Prim, prime	first
Psych	mind, soul
Pyro	fire
Rupt	break
Sat, satis	enough
Scrib, script	write
Sen	old
Sequ, secu, sue	follow
Serv	save, serve
Sign, signi	sign,mark,seal
Simil, simul	like, resemble
Skopeo	see, look
Sol	sun
Solus	alone
Sonus	sound

Spec, spect, spic	look
Tele	far away
Tempo	time
Ten, tin, tain	hold
Terra	earth
Therm	heat
Tom	cut
Tort, tors	twist
Tox	poison
Trans	across
Turbo	disturb
Typ	print
Uni	one
Urbs, Urbis	city
Verbum	word
Vert, vers	turn
Vict, vinc	conquer

Vid, vis	see
Vor	eat greedily
Zo, zoon	animal

CONTINENTS

Asia

Africa

North America

South America

Antarctica

Europe

Australia

STATES AND CAPITALS

Alabama	Montgomery
Alaska	Juneau
Arizona	Phoenix
Arkansas	Little Rock
California	Sacramento
Colorado	Denver
Connecticut	Hartford
Delaware	Dover
Florida	Tallahassee
Georgia	Atlanta
Hawaii	Honolulu
Idaho	Boise
Illinois	Springfield
Indiana	Indianapolis
Iowa	Des Moines
Kansas	Topeka

Kentucky	Frankfurt
Louisiana	Baton Rouge
Maine	Augusta
Maryland	Annapolis
Massachusetts	Boston
Michigan	Lansing
Minnesota	St Paul
Mississippi	Jackson
Montana	Helena
Nebraska	Lincoln
Nevada	Carson City
New Hampshire	Concord
New Jersey	Trenton
New Mexico	Santa Fe
New York	Albany
North Carolina	Raleigh
North Dakota	Bismarck

Ohio	Columbus
Oklahoma	OklahomaCity
Oregon	Salem
Pennsylvania	Harrisburg
Rhode Island	Providence
South Carolina	Columbia
South Dakota	Pierre
Tennessee	Nashville
Texas	Austin
Utah	SaltLakeCity
Vermont	Montpelier
Virginia	Richmond
Washington	Olympia
West Virginia	Charleston
Wisconsin	Madison
Wyoming	Cheyenne

THE STAR SPANGLED BANNER
By Francis Scott Key

Oh, say can you see, by the dawn's early light,

What so proudly we hailed at the twilight's last gleaming,

Whose broad stripes and bright stars, through the perilous fight,

O'er the ramparts we watched, were so gallantly streaming?

And the rocket's red glare, the bombs bursting in air,

Gave proof through the night that our flag was still there.

Oh say, does that Star-Spangled Banner yet wave

O'er the land of the free and the home of the brave?

AMERICA THE BEAUTIFUL
By
Katherine Lee Bates

O' beautiful, for spacious skies,

For amber waves of grain,

For purple mountain majesties,

Above the fruited plain.

America! America! God shed His grace on thee,

And crown thy good with brotherhood,

From sea to shining sea!

GOD BLESS AMERICA
By
Irving Berlin

God bless America,

Land that I love,

Stand beside her, and guide her,

Through the night, with a light from above.

From the mountains, to the prairies,

To the oceans, white with foam,

God Bless America,

My home, sweet home.

PLEDGE OF ALLEGIANCE
By Francis Bellamy

I pledge allegiance to the Flag of the United States of America,

And to the Republic for which it stands,

One Nation under God, indivisible,

With liberty and justice for all.

MY COUNTRY, 'TIS OF THEE
By Samuel F. Smith

My country, 'tis of thee,
Sweet land of liberty,
Of thee I sing.
Land where my fathers died,
Land of the pilgrims' pride,
From every mountain side,
Let freedom ring!

ERAS IN HISTORY

<u>Stone Age</u>.

<u>Bronze Age, 3200BC-1200BC</u>.
Stonehenge was built. Egypt began.

<u>Iron Age 1200BC-332BC</u>.

Trojan War was fought.

First Olympic games were played.

Famous people: Alexander the Great

Socrates

Aristotle

<u>Hellenistic Period 332BC-63BC</u>.

Alexander the Great took over Egypt and made it part of the Persian Empire.

Famous People: Julius Caesar

Cleopatra

Roman Period 63BC-476. Pompeii, Hadrian's Wall.

Famous People: Attila the Hun.

Middle Ages 476-1350. The Crusades; the Black Death in Europe.

Famous People: Genghis Khan

Marco Polo

Renaissance 1350-1600. Means rebirth; rebirth of culture, religion, education, art, and economics.

Famous People: Columbus

Leonardo da Vinci

Copernicus

Magellan

Martin Luther

<u>Reformation 1500-1600</u>. The rise up against the Catholic Church. People wanted the right to choose their religion and not be Catholic just because the government said so.

Famous People: Martin Luther, Saxom Monk; leader of the reformation in Germany. Wrote the "95 Theses Against Indulgences."

Sir Francis Drake

William Shakespeare

<u>Industrial Revolution 1750-1900</u>. The period where manufacturing changed from manual labor to machine labor and the energy source used for manufacturing

changed from wind, water, and animal to steam.

Other Events: The American Revolution

The French Revolution

The Eiffel Tower

Famous People: Marie Antoinette

Mozart

Napoleon Bonaparte

Beethoven

Darwin; Theory of Evolution

Van Gogh

Albert Einstein

Joseph Stalin

Mussolini

Adolf Hitler

<u>World War I 1914-1918</u>. Started with the assassination of the heir to the Austrian throne, Franz Ferdinand. Germany, Austria, and Hungary fought against Great Britain, France, Russia, Italy, Japan, and the U.S.

Famous People:

> John J. Pershing
>
> Vladimir Lenin
>
> Woodrow Wilson

<u>World War II 1939-1945</u>. Germany invades Poland. France and Great Britain declare war on Germany. Italy declared war against France and Britain (1940). U.S. provides aid to Britain (1941). In 1941 U.S. declares war on Japan. Germany and other Axis Powers declare war on U.S.

Famous People/Events:

Adolf Hitler

Albert Einstein

Atomic Bomb

Douglas MacArthur

Dwight D. Eisenhower

Franklin D. Roosevelt

George S. Patton

Joseph Stalin

Monuments Men

Mussolini

Nazi Party

Pearl Harbor

The Holocaust

Tuskegee Airmen

Winston Churchill

<u>Cold War 1945-1991</u>. Distrust between Russia and America; never fighting each other directly but fighting for their beliefs through other countries; example: Vietnam War. America had the atom bomb, and Russia had the most powerful army, and both were super powers. They knew that if they fought each other directly, it would be disastrous.

Other Event: Cuban Missile Crisis, 1962.

<u>Korean War 1950-1953</u>. War between democratic South Korea and the U.S. and communistic North Korea and China. North Korea invaded South Korea. America, United Kingdom, and 19 other countries aided South Korea with men and materials. The Soviet Union aided North Korea and China with materials.

Famous People: Dwight D. Eisenhower

Douglas MacArthur

<u>Vietnam War 1955-1975</u>. North Vietnam was communist and fought South Vietnam, anticommunist. The North was supplied by Russia and China, and the South was supplied with men and materials by the U.S.

<u>Desert Storm 1990-1991</u>. Iraq invaded Kuwait and took control of the country. America got involved to keep Iraq from invading Saudi Arabia and all of its oil. The U.S., United Kingdom, Egypt, and 32 other nations fought against Iraq.

<u>Afghanistan 2001-present</u>. "Operation Enduring Freedom." America, Australia, France, United Kingdom, and Afghan

United Front fought to get rid of the terrorists and the Taliban--who were responsible for taking down the Twin Towers in New York City (911)—and give Afghanistan back to the people.

Famous People: Al-Qaeda

Osama bin Laden

George Bush

References:

www.About.comAncient/Classical History

www.Ask.com/wiki/History-by-period

LANGUAGES

FRENCH

English	French	Pronounced
Hello	bonjour	bon-zhoor
Good night	bonne nuit	bon-newee
Please	s'il vous plait	see-vou-play
Thank you	merci	mare-see
Yes	oui	wee
No	no	
Great!	Grand!	
Beautiful	beau	bow
Delicious	delicieux	day-lee-see-uh
Bread	pain	pan

I would like.

  Je voudrais.

  zhuh-voo-dray

Excuse me.

Excusez-moi.

Excusum-mwa

Do you speak English?

Parlez vous anglais?

Parlay voo anglay?

Where is?

Ou est?

oo ay?

Where are the toilets?

Ou sont les toilettes?

Oo sohn lay twa-let?

How much is that?

Combien sont cela?

Comb-bee-yan-sone sell-ah?

I don't know.

Je ne sais pas.

Zhuh nuh say pah.

This is beautiful.

C'est beau.

Say bow.

Could you help me, please?

Sil vous plait pourriez vous maider?
See vou play poor-ee-ay vou may-day?

I'm going to.

Je vais a.

Zhuh vay ah.

Where is a bakery?

Ou est une boulangerie?

Ooo ay un boo-lonsh-a-ree?

How are you?

Ca va?   Sah-vah?

My name is.

Je m'appelle.

Shum eh pell.

These are my friends.

Ceux-ci-sont mes amis.

So see son mez-a-me.

I would like something to eat.

Je voudrais manjer quelque chose.
Shay voo dray mon-shay kell-koo
shows.

I would like something to drink.

Je voudrais boire quelque chose.

Shay voo-dray bwah kell-koo shows.

"Rick Steves' French, Italian, and German
Phrase Book."

SPANISH

English	Spanish	Pronounced
Hello	hola	oh-la
Good night	buenas nocher	
	bwain-ohs no-chez	
Please	por favor	poor fah-vor
Thank you	gracias	gracias
Yes	si	see
No	no	
Great!	Granday!	
Beautiful	hermoso	hair-moes-oh
Delicious	deliciose	
Bread	pan	
Where	donde?	doen-day?

How much is this?

    Cuanto vale esto?

    Quanto valay-stoe?

Excuse me.

    Pedoneme

    par-don-eh-me

Do you speak English?

    Habla ingles?

    A-blah English?

Where are the bathrooms?

    Donde estan los servicios?

    Doen-day ess-stan low servee-see-ohs?

How much is this?

    Cuanto vale esto?

    Quanto valay-stoe?

I don't know.

No se.   No say.

I would like.

Me gusta ria.

Me goost-a-ria.

This is beautiful.

Este es hermoso.

Estay es hair-moos-oh.

Can you help me, please?

Por favor ayudeme podea oustead?

Poor-fa-vor ah-do-a-may?

I would like to go to—

Me gustaria ir a.

Me goose-star-ia ear ah.

Where is a bakery?

Donde esta una panadera?

Done-day est una panadaria?

How are you?

Que tal?

Kay-tal?

My name is.

Me llamo.

Me lam-oh.

These are my friends.

Estos son mis amigos.

Estoe sun mees a-mee-goes.

I would like something to drink.

Me gustaria also beber.

May goose-star-ia also bear
bear.

I would like something to eat.

    Me gustaria also comer.

    May goose-star-ia algo comera.

GERMAN

English	German	Pronounced
Hello	hallo	hollow
Good night	gute nacht	goot-a-not
Please	bitte	bitta
Thank you	Danke	Don-ka
Yes	ja	ya
No	nein	nine
Great	Grob	Gross
Beautiful	schon	chun
Delicious	lecker	
Bread	brot	

English (Italic); German; Sounds Like:

How much is it?

Wie viel kostet das?

Vee feel cos-tet dahs?

Excuse me.

Entschuldigen sie mich.

In-shoel-ding zee mick.

Do you speak English?

Sprechen sie englisch?

Shprehk-in-zee ehng-lish?

Where is?

Wo ist?

Vo ist?

Where are the bathrooms?

Wo die badezimmer sind?

Vo dee bah-da-zimmer zent?

I don't know.

Ich weib nicht.

Eesh view neecht.

I would like.

Ich hatte gern.

Eek-heht-the gehrn.

I would like to go.

Ich mochte dazu gehen.

Eesh moistah dah soo gee-in.

Can you help me, please?

Bitta konnen sie mir helfen?

This is beautiful.

Das ist schon.

Das east chun.

Where is a bakery?

Wo ist backereist?

Vo ist back-er-eye?

How are you?

Wie sie sind?

Vee zee zent?

My name is.

Ich heibe.

Eek hi-she.

These are my friends.

Diese sind meine freunde.

Deeza zind mine ah froinda.

I would like something to drink.

Ich mochte dass etwas trank.

Eesh may-shta dass etvass tonk.

I would like something to eat.

Ich mochte dass etwas ab.

Eech may-shta etvass aus.

"Rick Steves' French, Italian, and German Phrase Book," and thanks to my German niece, Siggy.

Language Courses on DVD:
Dragonfly Language Video Flashcards.

52 Weeks of Family French: Bite Sized Weekly Lessons Designed to Get You and Your Family Speaking French Today by Eileen McAree.

Pimsleur Languages (one of my favorites).

Little PIM Fun With Languages.

Brainy Baby.

Foreign Languages for Kids by Kids:
Spanish Volume 1, 2, 3.

Muzzy BBC.

HEALTHY EATING

WHAT IS A GMO ANYWAY?

A GMO is a *Genetically Modified Organism.* So what does this mean? Well, let me explain a little better. In our grocery stores, in almost everything we eat and drink, we are ingesting GMOs. Scientists will take a regular seed and mutate it in a lab so it will grow larger, faster, and be more disease tolerant. A GMO plant cannot reproduce itself. It has to be created in a lab. There are 26 countries that have banned GMOs because of the health risks associated with these products.

Not only has it been taken from its natural state, but it is also fertilized with an unhealthy oil product. The product is so bad that the towns that grow these products shut down the drinking water systems at the time of year when they fertilize these plants because of the runoff from this product. It will cause a condition in humans called "blue baby syndrome." This is a condition that starves the body of oxygen and can effect babies as well as children and adults. It also depletes the soil of the natural occurring nutrients it has, therefore making our food less nutritious.

Most corn products, cottonseed, soybeans, and sugar beets are GMOs. Guess what?! These products are in almost every processed food you eat. They are in all our drinks, most all of the processed food we buy, and they are fed to cows, chickens, and pigs; so, in other words, in all meats. Our bodies are full of these products.

GMOs are very unhealthy for us and should be avoided, but HOW? GMOs are everywhere! To get started, buy as little processed food as possible. Try to eat fast food as little as possible. Shop on the outside perimeter of the grocery store. Buy products that are produced overseas. Most grocery stores have an aisle for these products. Buy organic when you can afford it. Join an organic food co-op. Be a label reader.

If we band together and stop buying these products, the FDA (the Government) will get the message and stop producing them. This is America, and we should not be poisoned by the foods we eat every day. This is a web site that will give you more information about GMOs: gmo-awareness.com.

I took everything out of my kitchen cabinets one day and read the labels. Ninety-five percent of the food and drinks had GMO products in them. That is really scary.

When you say the word "organic," most people think of no taste and high prices. Back in the day, organic meant bean sprouts, tofu, seaweed, and just plain weird food. Well, times have changed. Today any food you normally buy can now be found as organic.

What does "organic" mean? It is food that has not been sprayed with poisonous toxins. It has to be made with non-GMO products, and the meat and dairy animals have to be fed non-GMO feed.

Recently the word "Natural" has popped up on many food packages and products, but don't let that mislead you. With the natural labels, the company can still use GMO products and feed their animals GMO feed. Always look for the "organic" or "non-GMO" label. It will be proudly displayed.

At this time, COSTCO and Earth Fare carry the best selection of organic foods. More and more suppliers are bringing in organic foods, and for that we are very thankful.

Organic does cost a little more, but it is not as much as you think. I took a good friend shopping one day, and she was shocked at the cost when I checked out. It was a lot lower than she thought it would be. I cook a lot, and I'm talking real meals. We eat at home most of the time.

Look at it this way. You can pay a little more now or a lot more later in doctor bills for bad health. In my family, after eating organic and non-GMO foods, various members have seen an improvement in weight loss, fibromyalgia, cholesterol, kidney function, diabetes, and high blood pressure. We started to see the first improvements after about six weeks. I think this is an awesome testimony for eating healthy.

This will not be an easy challenge. Getting used to shopping for organic takes a while, but once you get the hang of it, it becomes as easy as your old way of shopping

My daughter had to be on bed rest during her third pregnancy for about three weeks. I went to her house every day and most of the time made lunch while I was there. She could not get over how easy I made it seem to make real nutritional meals with real food. She was a good cook but she seldom made meals from total scratch because she thought it would take forever and be a lot of trouble.

After seeing how easy it was, she asked me to go grocery shopping with her after the baby was born and help her stock her pantry with all the appropriate ingredients for a wholesome kitchen. So off we went to the store and here is a list of what we bought. NOTE: This is a lot of food, but once your pantry is initially stocked, you only replace what has been used.

DAIRY

Eggs – organic and/or cage free.

Butter – not margarine; it's high in trans fats; it is fake, a man-made product. There is salted and unsalted butter.

Cream cheese – don't buy products that have "less fat" in them. They just replace the fat with some other man-made ingredient. Also, researchers have found that low fat products actually make you gain weight.

Milk – Buy whole milk.

Sour cream.

Heavy cream.

Cheese, not shredded.

Yogurt – Greek is best.

BAKING GOODS

Baking soda.

Baking powder.

Brown sugar.

Flour – don't buy enriched and bleached flour.

Yeast.

Cornmeal.

Chocolate chips.

Sugar.

Cocoa powder.

PRODUCE--A farmers' market is best.

Onions.

Peppers.

Mushrooms.

Cabbage.

Lettuce.

Bananas.

Garlic.

Potatoes.

Grapes.

Squash.

Tomatoes.

Cucumbers.

Don't buy too much or it will spoil. Anything seasonal is best. The fresher the better!!

Your favorite fruit.

CANNED GOODS

Beans – green, kidney, pink, pinto.

Soups – cream of mushroom, cream of chicken.

Tomato sauce.

Peas.

Corn – cream and whole; have only found organic whole corn.

Pears.

Apples.

Water chestnuts.

Stewed tomatoes.

Tuna, wild caught.

<u>DRIED GOODS.</u> The dried beans and peas are not organic but are non-GMO.

White lima beans.

Black-eyed peas.

Quick oats.

Pasta.

Italian bread crumbs.

Grits.

Tortillas (flour).

Croutons.

Ritz crackers (the organic kind won't be the Ritz brand).

Rice.

Tea bags.

SEASONINGS, SPREADS, OILS

Garlic salt.

Sea salt.

Vanilla.

Black pepper.

Olive oil – best.

Organic Canola oil – next best.

Mayo.

Peanut butter.

Jelly.

Taco seasoning package.

Lipton onion soup mix.

Chili seasoning package.

Ketchup.

Worcestershire sauce.

Spaghetti sauce.

Picante sauce.

Chicken stock.

MEAT

Hamburger – as lean as you can afford.

Whole chicken.

Cut up chicken – I like bone-in skin-on. It has more flavor.

Canned chicken.

Hot dogs.

Fish; wild caught salmon is a favorite.

FROZEN VEGETABLES

Petite baby limas.

Breaded okra.

Petite baby carrots.

Blueberries.

French fries.

Corn on the cob.

BREAD

French.

Italian.

Whole wheat.

Crescent rolls.

Biscuits.

<u>Suggested dinner menus for two weeks:</u>

1. Meat loaf, mashed potatoes, glazed carrots.

2. Fried chicken, deviled eggs, mashed potatoes.

3. Roasted chicken, vegetable casserole, fried okra.

4. Lasagna, green salad, Italian or French bread.

5. Chili, cornbread, green salad.

6. Sloppy Joe's, French fries, pear salad.

7. Chicken casserole, green beans, corn casserole.

8. Spaghetti, salad, drop biscuits.

9. Barbecue chicken, black-eyed peas, potato salad.

10. Pig in a blanket, French fries, stewed apples.

11. Chicken and rice, squash, petite baby lima beans.

12. Pizza, salad.

13. Taco's.

14. Tuna casserole, green salad, rolls.

FAVORITE FAMILY RECIPES

UNCOOKED COOKIES

2 cups sugar
1 stick butter
1/3 cup peanut butter
1/3 cup cocoa
1/2 cup milk
3 cups Quick Oats

Bring all ingredients, except oats, to a boil and boil for one minute. Remove from heat and stir in oats. Drop by spoonsful onto waxed paper. They will then harden. My family really likes them.

CHOCOLATE CHIP CHEESE BALL

1 8-oz package cream cheese
1 cup mini-chocolate chips from a 12-oz bag
1/2 cup powdered sugar
1/4 cup butter, softened
1/2 tsp vanilla extract
1 cup chopped pecans

Combine all ingredients, mixing well. Shape mixture into a ball. Roll in the remaining chocolate chips. Serve with gingersnap cookies or vanilla wafers.

IRON SKILLET APPLE PIE

1 stick butter
¾ cup brown sugar
1 cup granulated white sugar
2 pie crusts (I use frozen)
2 tsp cinnamon
4 lg or 6 small Granny Smith apples
    (or fresh pears) thinly sliced

Preheat oven to 350 degrees. Place butter in large iron skillet and melt in the oven. Remove from oven and stir in brown sugar and let melt. Place first pie crust on top of brown sugar and press up sides of skillet. Mix white sugar and cinnamon. Place apples over pie crust; sprinkle white sugar mixture over apples. Now place second pie crust over apples. Pinch the two crusts together as much as possible. With sharp knife, pierce pie crust 4-6 times. Bake until golden brown. *It is the best apple/pear pie I have ever eaten.*

BAKLAVA--A GREEK DESSERT

Phyllo sheets
1 cup melted butter
2 cups chopped nuts
1/2 cup sugar
1/2 tsp cinnamon

Syrup
3/4 cup sugar
3/4 cup honey
1 cup water
1 table spoon lemon juice

Put phyllo sheets in casserole dish one at the time. Brush sheet with butter, sprinkle with nuts, sugar, and cinnamon. Repeat until you run out of ingredients. Put remaining phyllo sheets (5 or 6) on top of dish, brush with butter. Bake at 400 until brown and crisp, about 30 minutes.

While this is baking, mix the syrup. Put all ingredients in a pot and boil on top of stove for about 15 minutes. Cool the syrup and pour over Baklava.

COLD BANANA PUDDING

3 boxes vanilla pudding (instant)
5 cups milk
8 oz sour cream
1/2 of a large Coolwhip
1 box vanilla wafers
6 bananas

Mix pudding and milk. Add sour cream and Coolwhip, mixing well. Layer cookies, bananas, and pudding until all is used. Top with rest of Coolwhip.

EASY FRUIT COBBLER

You will need a pan that can be used on top of stove and in the oven.

Put your favorite fruit--blueberries, peaches, etc--in bottom of pan.
Add one stick butter.
Use enough water to just cover bottom of pan.
3/4 cup sugar.

When butter and sugar are melted and mixed with water and fruit, bring to a boil. As it gently boils, pinch off pieces of canned biscuit dough and drop into mixture. Top with sugar.

Transfer pan to oven and bake at 350 until golden brown.

CHICKEN AND RICE CASSEROLE

One can cream of chicken soup
1/2 cup mayo
1/4 cup milk
1 Tablespoon lemon juice
1/4 tsp salt
3 boiled eggs, chopped
2 cups cooked chicken, chopped
1 cup regular rice, cooked
1 can chopped water chestnuts, drained
1 small jar diced pimiento
1/2 cup celery, chopped
1 tablespoon onion, finely chopped
1/3 cup crushed corn flakes
1/4 cup slivered almonds
1 tablespoon butter, melted

Combine first 5 ing; add next 7 ing. Mix well.
Place in greased casserole dish. Combine
corn flakes, almonds, and butter. Sprinkle
over casserole and bake at 325 until bubbly,
about 30 minutes.

CROCKPOT CAMP STEW

2 cans whole kernel corn
2 cans diced tomatoes
1 8- to 12-oz bottle ketchup
2 10-oz cans of chicken
1 pound ground beef, cooked
1 tablespoon Worcestershire sauce
2 cans potatoes, diced

Place in crockpot and simmer on low all day or about 4 hours on high.

GNOCCHI
(Pronounced nokie)

6 medium potatoes
1 egg
flour
1/2 tsp salt
dash of pepper
milk

Butter sauce:
1/2 cup butter
1 clove garlic
Parmesan cheese, grated

Boil and mash potatoes with a small amount of milk the day before; cover and refrigerate for 24 hours. Remove potatoes; add egg, salt, and pepper. Add flour as needed to make a non- sticky dough. Knead dough for 5 minutes. Roll pieces of dough on floured surface into a "snake or rope," approximately 1/4-inch thick. Cut into 1/2-inch pieces. Boil large pan of salted water. Add gnocchi, a few at a time. When they rise to the top, remove with a slotted spoon and place on platter. Use all of them. To make sauce: Melt butter, add garlic. Pour over gnocchi. Sprinkle with Parmesan cheese.

This dish is a little messy and time consuming, but the results are to die for.

Recipe by Freda Colestro from the cookbook, "A Bit of Italy."

ITALIAN BREAD

1 ¼ cup warm water
1 pkg active dry yeast
1 ½ tsp salt
3 cups unsifted all-purpose flour

Pour water into warm mixing bowl. Sprinkle yeast over it, and stir to dissolve. Add salt. Stir in 2 cups flour. Turn out on floured board; knead in enough flour to make a smooth, elastic dough.

Place dough in an oiled bowl, turning to coat with oil. Cover; let rise in warm place until it has doubled in size—about 1 ½ hours. Punch down and let rise again, about 1 hour. Punch down and turn dough out on lightly floured board. Shape into a long loaf. Let rise 1 ½ hours. Heat oven to 400 and bake until brown, about 40 minutes.

This is an easy and inexpensive recipe and makes great Italian bread.

MEXICAN CASSEROLE

1 lb ground beef, cooked and drained
1 jar picante sauce

1 8-oz pkg cream cheese

1 8-oz sour cream
1 15-oz can pinto beans, drained
1 15-oz can of corn, drained
1 pkg taco seasoning
2 cups cheese
2 boxes Jiffy corn meal mix
2 eggs
2/3 cup milk

You will need a pan that can be used on top of stove and in the oven. Mix all ingredients together except the last three, and simmer on top of stove. Mix the meal, eggs, and milk and place on top of meat mixture. Place pan in oven and bake at 350 until golden brown.

MA-MA'S TEA CAKES
(Sugar Cookies)

1 cup shortening
1 3/4 cup sugar
2 eggs
3 cups flour
2 tsp baking powder
1/2 tsp salt
1/2 cup milk

Cream shortening and sugar; add eggs. Add dry ingredients alternately with milk. It works better to put the dough in fridge for at least an hour or until you are ready to make them. Take out of fridge and place on floured surface. Mix with your hands, and add a little flour as you knead dough until it's not sticky. Roll out and cut with cookie cutters. Bake at 350 until light brown.

GRANNY'S ARTICHOKE DIP

1 can artichoke hearts, drained. Place in
    blender and blend.
1 cup mayo
1 cup Parmesan cheese
1 tsp garlic powder
1 tsp dill weed
2 8-oz blocks cream cheese
a sprinkle of red pepper

Mix all ingredients. Place in a medium sized
baking dish and sprinkle the top with a little
red pepper. Bake at 350 for 30-35 minutes.
Serve warm with crackers or chips.

This recipe is a huge hit at parties.

CHICKEN CASSEROLE
(Poppy Seed)

4 chicken breasts, boiled then shredded.
    (I prefer bone-in because of better flavor)
2 cans cream of chicken soup
1 8-oz sour cream
Ritz crackers
1/2 stick butter
1 tsp poppy seeds

Put chicken in casserole dish. Sprinkle garlic salt and pepper for your taste. Mix soup and sour cream together and pour over chicken. Crumble one or two tubes of Ritz crackers over mixture. (I place crackers in ziplock bag and crush by rolling a glass or rolling pin over crackers.) Sprinkle poppy seeds over crackers. Bake at 350 for 30 minutes. Ten minutes before it's done, pour butter over crackers.

MOM'S SPAGHETTI SAUCE

1 1/2 lbs ground beef, browned and drained
1 14-15 oz can diced tomatoes
1 8-oz can tomato sauce
    Using the same can to measure, add
        1 can ketchup
        1 can water
1 can cream of mushroom soup
1 large onion, diced
1 large bell pepper, diced
2 heaping teaspoons sugar
Salt and pepper to taste
Optional: 1 box fresh sliced mushrooms

After meat is browned and drained, add all ingredients and simmer about 3 hours or in a crockpot all day on low. Serve over spaghetti noodles.

FETTUCINE ALFREDO
by Deborah DiPofi

4 tsps olive oil

4 tsps finely chopped garlic

1 lb fettucine, cooked

6 cups heavy whipping cream or half and half

12 egg yolks

8 tblspns Parmesan cheese

Salt and pepper to taste

Sautee garlic in oil for 20 seconds, then add pasta and toss. Next, add cream and reduce by 2/3. Add half of the cheese. Remove from heat and add egg yolks and stir. Season to taste. When serving, add remaining cheese.

"A Bit of Italy" cookbook by the American Italian Association of Montgomery, Alabama.

Some parts of the recipe have been altered to better suit my family's taste.

This recipe is from www.yummly.com. It is The Old Spaghetti Factory's Creamy Pesto Salad Dressing Recipe. I tweaked it a little bit so it is not exactly the same.

HOMEMADE SALAD DRESSING

1 cup mayo

1 ¼ cups buttermilk

1 ½ tbsps fresh basil leaves, finely chopped

1 tsp minced garlic, finely chopped

½ tsp garlic salt

1/8 tsp pepper

½ cup parmesan cheese, finely shredded

When I finished mixing, I poured 2 or 3 tbsps of olive oil in to make it not so thick. Mix ings in a bowl, or you may use a blender. With something like this, tweak to your taste.

Cooking Terms:

Fold—Gently turn ingredients with spoon or spatula until well blended; i.e., coolwhip and soft jello mixture. Start at bottom of bowl and bring up and over until ingredients are well blended.

Cut in—When mixing butter or shortening into flour, some recipes will say "cut in ingredients." To do this, use a pastry cutter or two knives (one in each hand) slicing back and forth until mixture is about the size of peas. With a pastry cutter, rock it back and forth until properly cut in.

Whisk—Use a whisk or fork to beat; for instance, eggs or egg whites until smooth.

Baste—Spoon liquid over food periodically while baking; for instance, spoon turkey broth (that cooks out of the turkey) over turkey to keep it moist and juicy.

Measure—Dry ingredients: flour, sugar, corn meal, nuts, etc. Place in a cup and level off with a knife.

Measure wet ingredients: milk, water, oil, etc. with a (usually) clear measuring cup; most have a spout for easy pouring and measurements on side of cup.

Use the freshest ingredients available.

Use unbleached flour. It is better for you and makes cookies rise much better.

Buy baking soda at the health food store. This soda does not have aluminum in it.

Softened butter is not melted butter but butter that has been allowed to reach room temperature to become soft.

Blanch—Put food (usually vegetables) into boiling water for two or three minutes. This will preserve color, keep in nutrition, and help remove skin from some fruits and tomatoes. You can also do this to a chicken before plucking its feathers.

Caramelize—Two ways: One, bring out the food's own natural sugar; for example, onions. Cook in sauté pan until the sugar begins to cook out of them, making them sweet and tasty. When onions begin to brown and plump, they will be ready. Another way is by putting brown sugar and butter in a pan with carrots, for example. Cook over medium heat until a light brown syrup begins to coat the carrots.

Deglaze—After frying food in a pan, remove the food. Pour a liquid such as broth, wine, or water over any fat or oil left in the pan. This mixes with the bits of food and drippings and makes a gravy or sauce.

GARDENING

GARDENING

It's that time of year again! Time to roll up those sleeves and get your hands dirty. So why have a vegetable garden, you ask? Why not?!! It's great exercise, fun for the whole family, and has hands-on science written all over it; and to top it all off, in the end you get fresh, nutritious, fruits and vegetables that taste better than anything you can buy in a grocery store.

In science we studied about the nutritional value of foods produced today versus the nutritional value of foods produced 60 years ago. Our soil has become so nutritionally depleted that in order to get the same nutrition today, we would have to consume three to four times as many vegetables and fruits to equal the nutritional value from a regular serving from 60 years ago.

In other words, today we're eating empty calories and not getting the nutrition we should be getting from our food. Also, if you grow your food organically, you don't have to worry about pesticides that could harm your family, so it's a win-win situation.

Let's get started by discussing the different kinds of vegetables. Vegetables are broken down into families, and the families should be planted together. So here they are in alphabetical order.

<u>Alliums</u>: onions, scallions, shallots, garlic, and leeks.

<u>Brassicas</u>: cabbage, kale, broccoli, cauliflower, brussel sprouts, mustard, radishes, turnips, collards, and rutabagas.

<u>Cucurbits</u>: cucumbers, melons, and all squash from zucchini to pumpkins and gourds.

<u>Gramineae</u>: corn.

<u>Legumes</u>: beans, peas, and peanuts.

<u>Malvaceae</u>: okra.

<u>Mescluns</u>: endive, escarole, swiss chard, shicory, arugula, and radiccio lettuce.

<u>Solanaceae</u>: tomatoes, peppers, eggplant, potatoes.

<u>Umbelliferae</u>: celery, carrot, dill, chervil, cilantro, parsley, fennel, and parsnip.

These families should be planted in the same bed because they use soil in the same way and also have similar pests. The key to a healthy garden is to rotate these families every year. This helps to keep the soil rich with nutrients, free from diseases, and will also keep pests to a minimum. Perennials, like asparagus and herbs, are the only crops that don't need rotating.

Rotate the plant family so it will not be in the same bed more often than every four years, if space allows. When you are planning your beds, keep this in mind. Also, put your beds in a spot that gets six to eight hours of sun per day.

Raised beds are easier and better for your plants. They keep the soil warmer during colder weather, improve drainage, and keep the soil from becoming hard and compacted. Make your raised beds 8-12 inches deep and just wide enough that you don't have to step on the soil when working them. Don't use old creosote railroad ties or treated lumber because they are toxic and not good for your plants or your family.

Fill the beds with composted soil and amend them with cow, chicken, rabbit, and horse manure for a great, healthy, organic fertilizer. Use layers of newspaper (no colored inserts) and straw or hay between garden rows and under and between plants to help keep weeds down and moisture up.

It's also a great idea to put earthworms in the soil, if it doesn't already have them. You will find the worms where fish bait is sold. Buy a few containers and sprinkle them in the soil. They are inexpensive and great for keeping the soil aeriated and rich with nutrients.

Okay, now that you have figured out what you want to grow and where your beds will be and how to have healthy, happy soil, let's talk about organic gardening. The definition of an organic garden is one free of synthetic chemicals. This includes pesticides, synthetic fertilizers, and non-organic seeds or plants. Organic gardening is the oldest, cheapest, healthiest, and most practical way of growing vegetables.

Usually when men alter what God has made, something is not healthy or safe about it. One example: You cannot save the seed of a hybrid plant to use for the next year. With organic plants, you can save your seed for the next year's planting.

So let's get your beds ready for planting. In a nice, clean, weed-less bed--and before planting season--plant wheat, oats, rye, or French marigolds. Then a few weeks prior to planting your vegetables, turn them under and into the soil. This will reduce the nematode (a harmful pest) population. You can also grow mustard or horseradish between crops and turn them under. Not only does this suppress the pest population, but it increases production of tomatoes, potatoes, and eggplant.

If you have a raised bed that has unhealthy soil caused by bacteria, fungi, or pests, you can solarize it. During the hottest part of the year, put plastic over the bed. The heat from the sun through the plastic will raise the temperature of the soil so high that bacteria, fungi, and pests are unable to survive.

Last but not least, if you will break up/turn/till the soil two or three times before planting, you will have a less weedy garden. This is also a good time to put fresh compost and manure in the bed.

Now it's time to sow the seed and put out the plants. My Grandmother's rule of thumb is to plant your garden on Good Friday. You can always plant it after that but never before that. Also, if the pecan tree leaves are budding out, the danger of frost is over so you don't have to worry about frost hurting your tender plants.

It's good to plant crops continually throughout the season instead of all at once. This way you are not bombarded with a thousand squash that you can't possibly eat, can, or freeze.

Soak okra seeds overnight before planting. This helps them come up faster because they have a hard, thick hull. You will see plants for sale of cucumbers, squash, and even melons; but from years of trial and error, starting from seed produces healthier and more productive plants. This is true for everything except tomato plants. They transplant quite well.

Running beans (pole beans) and peas need something vertical to grow on. This can be done by having fence wire fastened to poles;

by placing long poles in the ground and then running heavy string in an up and down pattern from pole to pole; by making a teepee of 6-8 foot poles and planting at the base of the poles; then there is the economical method of cutting tall, stout branches in the woods for the vines to grow on.

I have found that putting a bed along the fence line of the garden supplies ample space for running plants. Of course you have to have a fence around your garden, but I have found that to be not only a great thing to grow plants on but also pretty, and it keeps the dogs and cats and any other pests out of my garden.

Last but not least, you can also buy tomato cages for running beans and peas. Even cucumbers will grow vertically on a tomato cage. If you have room to plant corn, you can even plant peas and beans with the corn, and the peas will climb up the corn. Plant squash at the base of the corn plant to shade the roots and help prevent weeds. This gives you three vegetables to assist each other.

When planting tomatoes, an empty toilet paper roll can be placed over the plant and pressed into the ground to keep caterpillars away. Buy healthy tomato plants, but bigger is not better. In order to have a great root system, break off all the limbs (leaves) except the last four. Put the entire plant in the soil almost to the top limbs. If the plant is so tall that you can't dig the hole deep enough, lay the plant lengthwise, but always go as deep as possible. This will give you a strong, productive plant.

A good watering system for tomatoes is to put a large can or plastic bottle with the bottom cut out around the tomato when it is planted. Push a few inches into the ground. When you water the plant, water directly into the can or bottle. This sends the water directly to the roots rather than spreading over a large area. This really helps during droughts.

Another way that works is to place a gallon milk jug that has two or three holes in the bottom between or around the plants. The jug needs to be pushed into the soil a little ways in order to be stable. The water will gradually seep into the ground and to the plants. You can try both ways to see which works best for you. I prefer the container around the plant.

Rain or well water is best for your plants. Water that comes from the hose is chlorinated, and the plants just do not prosper as well when watered with this. If you have a good place for a rain barrel, that is also good to water your garden with.

You can put a whole-house filter on your water system, and this will give you non-chlorinated water for your house and garden, or you can buy a filter just for your hose. These are sold in some organic seed catalogs. A soaker hose is then recommended to water your garden. The plants get more deeply watered and produce stronger, healthier, and deeper roots. If you don't have a soaker hose, you can water with a sprinkler system or regular hose.

I like standing outside late in the afternoon or early in the morning watering my garden by hand. It is so therapeutic and relaxing. Just make sure the plants get at least one inch of water at the time so the soil gets deeply drenched and not just wet on the top.

A good way to gauge an inch of water is to put an empty tuna can in the garden, and when it's full, you have an inch. If you do this, you only have to water every three days. In other words, it's better to water thoroughly less often than to water a little every day.

If you want an attractive garden, plant herbs, vegetables, and flowers together. Flowers attract good insects that eat the bad insects. We always plant marigolds and sun flowers in our garden, along with a few others for color and pest control. Vegetables that taste great and are also pretty are sweet peas, endive, kale, red cabbage, and ruby chard.

Herbs are also a good pest control but they have a tendency to spread and multiply. To prevent this, plant them in a container in the garden or in a large container beside the garden. Herbs are a great addition to the garden and will add an array of flavor to your cooking and to your medicine cabinet.

To keep weeds at bay, hoe or use a weeding tool to get the weeds when they are just coming up. My favorite weeding tool is the one with a hoe handle attached to a u-shaped metal piece at the end. This tool slices right through the soil, pulling the weeds up as it goes. It is so easy and fast to use, and every one with flower beds or a garden needs this tool. You can buy it at most garden centers.

I have found that if you run this tool through your rows or beds in between the plants, you will not have a weed problem. But remember, do this when the weeds barely pop up from the soil. The more you do this, the less weeds you have as the season progresses.

You can also put mulch between and around plants. If you do this, it has to be real thick, and sometimes--or almost all the time-- in my garden the weeds battle right through it. By the time I see them, they are huge and I have to pull them by hand. Plus, I have to buy or find all that mulch. I find it easier just to use my weeding tool to have clean beds and rows.

Now after all the tips you have about organic gardening, if you are still having a pest problem, here are a few more things you can do. For slugs, cut the leaves off the bottom part of the plant and also pull off the leaves that have been damaged by the slug. You can put bark dust or more compost around the bottom of the plant.

Another trick that has been around for a long time is to fill a shallow container with beer (for the slugs, not you) and place in the garden at ground level. At night the slugs will come to it, crawl in, then die.

You can also use insecticidal soap approved by the OMRI. Look for the "OMRI Listed" seal on the container. This means it is truly an organic product. This product kills soft-bodied pests (aphids, mealy bugs, spider mites, and white flies) but not beneficial insects.

There is also Neem oil. Pests don't like the way it tastes; and if they do consume it, it messes up their molting and reproductive cycles. It's nontoxic to birds, mammals, and beneficial bugs. And last but not least, if your plant just refuses to grow, move it somewhere else in the garden. Each growing season will be different in the way plants perform, but don't give up; sharing a meal that you and your family have grown is fantastic, and it tastes so good!!

Finally, during the end of the growing season, you can extend your fall crops with a coat of straw over them. This will keep them warmer and producing longer. At the end of the season, be sure to remove all dead and decaying plants so insects won't have anywhere to live in the winter. Pull them up, chop them up, and turn them under; or put them in your compost pile. In the spring before planting, give your garden a good dose of fresh compost for a healthy and happy soil.

Just remember, a variety of plants and good healthy soil fed with organic compost and fertilizer will keep your garden at its best naturally. So get out there and have some fun with your family, learn a lot, and get on the road to a healthy way of life.

Oh, by the way; gardening for one hour burns 400 calories!!

CHICKENS

CHICKENS

That's right! And why not? Chickens are easy to raise, make great pets, fertilize your garden, and best of all provide fresh eggs!

We started raising chickens about two years ago. It took a lot of trial and error, mostly error, the first year, but we finally caught on and, WOW, do we love raising chickens.

My husband and I built our chicken pen. I saw one at someone's house and thought we could do that. I took pictures of it and showed it to my husband, and we built it! It took about three really hot summer mornings to get it done.

Our pen is made up of four landscape timbers cemented into the ground at each corner and two timbers on each side of the door and a timber on the opposite side of the door in the middle. Two by fours are nailed at the bottom, middle, and top around the entire cage. The door is also made of 2x4s built in the shape of a rectangle with a cross piece up top running diagonally and a cross piece in the middle and another one on the bottom running diagonally.

We dug a trench in the ground all the way around the pen so the chicken wire would go down into the ground so that animals could not dig under the wire to get to our chickens. Yes, we have seen the proverbial fox cross our yard now and then.

We also put a 2x4 across the top from front to back and side to side, then we wrapped the whole thing in chicken wire, even across the top. In other words, we built a box with a door and wrapped it in wire.

We built nesting boxes on the inside, but the chickens we have will lay their eggs everywhere but in the boxes. The boxes are not enclosed, so I think if we enclose them, they will lay in them.

I have hung rope from the top 2x4s and attached the chicken feeder and watering bucket to it. This keeps the food and water off the ground and keeps it clean and dry.

We got our first batch of chickens and ended up with five hens (girls) and one rooster (boy). The farm store will try to give you the sexes you want, but now and then you will get a surprise. It is very hard to tell what sex they are when they are babies.

By the way, you don't have to have a rooster to have eggs. Hens can lay eggs without any help from the male. If you want babies, then you must have a rooster. Sounds like a good idea, right. WRONG!!!! Roosters can be mean! We ate our rooster.

I decided to put an old plastic dog house in the pen for cover. Well, they started laying eggs in it. The floor was hard, and one got broken. The chickens got a taste of it and then started eating their eggs! We couldn't get them to stop, so we ate the chickens.

The next year we got nine hens. Thank goodness, no surprises. We got five Buff Orphingtons, the kittens of chickens; two Rhode Island Reds; and two Domineckers. All these breeds are gentle and make good pets, AND they lay really well. We get at least a dozen eggs every two days. The children love petting, feeding, and collecting the eggs. The hens are so gentle that the children can pick them up and hold them.

We put the chicken pen close to our garden, then we put a fence around the garden and connected it to the chicken pen. We can open the gate and into the garden they go. Chickens can clean out a garden so it's important to be able to control when they can go in. In the fall we let them in to scratch and get rid of weeds. They also fertilize the garden. The garden needs to be free of chickens three months before you plant. This allows the poop to compost and makes it safe to plant.

The second year we got our chickens, the babies kept dying. I researched the problem and finally found someone having the same problem. The chicken feed was too big. I started putting it in the blender and pulverizing it and had no more problems.

I always buy baby chicks because they are so cute. I keep them inside in a box with a heating pad under the box to keep them warm. I put shredded newspaper in the box and change it twice a day. At Easter you can even get colored chicks.

Last but not least, the eggs are sooo much better than what you buy. The yolks are a deep golden color, and the eggs taste fantastic! I only feed organic food to the chickens and attribute the wonderful eggs to that.

We had a funny situation with one hen who was "brooding." This means she thinks she has babies in the eggs, so she sits on them to make them hatch. She doesn't want you to collect them and gets very annoyed if you try to get the eggs from under her. Other hens will continue to lay in the same nest, and she wants to sit (colloquially, she is "setting) on them.

While I was on vacation with some female "hens," my husband, who doesn't like to be "hen pecked," came up with an ingenious way to collect the eggs. He got one of those "grabber sticks" and would gently put it under the hen and pull the eggs out one by one. Not only did I get a good laugh out of this, but it really worked!

Sometimes it becomes necessary to clip a chicken's wings because they can learn to fly. It is very easy to do this. First, hold the chicken upside down by her feet. Her wings will automatically fall outward and all the blood will rush to her head so she becomes very still for you. Look at the wing; there are two rows of feathers. The long ones on the outside are the ones you want to cut. Trim them about a third of the way off. This does not hurt the chicken at all.

I keep being amazed at how smart chickens really are. I made a makeshift gate from wire that curves around and sticks into the other side of the fence. It does not fasten here but is difficult to pull open.

I looked out my window and noticed that all my chickens were in the garden. I immediately blamed my grandchildren, thinking they had left the gate open. As I began to put my chickens up and was down to the last few, I noticed one of the chickens running towards the gate. She then put her head in one of the gate's square wire holes and kept running, using the weight of her body to push the gate open. I was shocked! She kept doing this until it opened enough for her and all her accomplices to escape. Luckily I saw it with my own eyes or I would have gotten onto three innocent little girls.

PHOTOGRAPHY

PHOTOGRAPHY

First let's go over the settings on your camera dial and find out what they mean and do.

P--this stands for program. If your camera setting is on this, your camera is in full automatic mode. It will set everything for you to get the proper picture.

TV--this mode lets you set your shutter speed, and the camera automatically sets everything else. This is great for capturing speed and motion. A low TV number (i.e., 30) gives you water that looks smooth and silky. You will need a tripod for this because the shutter stays open so long that it's impossible to hold the camera steady.

Set your camera at a high TV number (i.e., 1/500) for action shots such as your dog playing fetch, a soccer game, etc.

AV--this mode lets you set your own aperture or f-stop, and the camera will automatically set everything else. For a blurred background, set your f-stop to a low number such as 2.8. To take great scenery shots where everything in the picture is crisp and sharp, set your f-stop high (i.e., 29).

The Nikon camera's dial is a little different. M--is manual; you make all the decisions.

A--is aperture; you choose the aperture; camera does the rest.

S--is shutter speed; you choose shutter speed; camera does the rest.

P--is program; camera does it all; just point and shoot.

The pictures on your dial have a specific purpose:

A girl--this is the portrait mode; it makes skin look better, and subject is softer.

A mountain--this is the scenery mode. It keeps everything in the entire picture in focus. When shooting scenery, it's best to shoot horizontally; but remember, creativity has no rules!

A flower--this is the close-up mode. Use this to get up close and personal on the subject.

A stick man running--use this mode for fast action shots.

A man and a star on a black background--this mode is for capturing people at night.

A child--this mode is great for capturing children. They move and will not sit still during a shoot, and this will keep your pictures from being blurry and will give you the portrait mode effect.

Some cameras have a scene mode. This gives you even more options than what is on your dial. To set your scene mode, turn your dial to "scene." There is usually another small dial on the back of your camera to turn, and then you can see all your options.

Snowman--good for a shoot in the snow or on the beach; keeps your pictures from being too bright and washed out with the white snow or sand.

Sun--great for sunsets.

Building with Moon--night scapes.

Fork and Knife--shooting food.

Tree w/Leaf--great for fall leaves; intensifies the colors.

Candle flame--great for dark, candle-lit rooms or around a fire.

Last, but not least, the *effects mode*. This allows you to apply special effects to your photos so that you can get "artsy" and creative.

Photographing People

<u>Children</u>: Don't photograph them from above. Get down on their level. If you have a "child mode" on your camera, use it; or try putting your aperture on a low number for a blurred background. You can also try putting your camera's shutter speed to a high number if your subject is moving or playing. Try all three and see how different your pictures turn out. Also, remember to do some close-ups, full body, and profiles.

Try to capture your child's personality. Take shots of them smiling, serious, crying, whatever the moment presents. Remember that children can change expressions by the second, so you always have to be ready.

<u>Adults</u>: Move around the person to find an angle that flatters them. For older people, especially women, photograph them from above. This makes their face and neck area smoother and younger looking. Try to have a

neutral background, not too busy, so as to not distract from the subject.

You can put your aperture on a low number for the blurred effect. You can only achieve a certain amount of blur with certain lenses. For super blurred effects, you will need to buy a lens that has very low aperture numbers. If you are outside, shoot in the shade. If this is not possible, use your flash to remove harsh shadows from their face.

Photographers have two special times of day when the light outside is perfect: right before sunrise and right after sunset. This is called the golden light.

Make sure your subject is not standing or sitting in front of something that will look as if it were growing out of their head. Place your subject off center in a horizontal photo for more interest. Eliminate background shadow.

If your subject is standing in front of a building and is casting a shadow on it, place your subject five to seven feet away from the background. Take a lot of pictures at different angles and views. Eliminate "red eye" by having the subject NOT look directly into the camera.

When photographing groups, try to form shapes; for example, triangles, heart shapes, V shapes, etc., to provide more interest. Put your camera on A-dep mode to keep everyone in focus. If you don't have A-dep, put it on the mode with a mountain on it. This will keep everything in focus.

The best lighting inside is natural light from a window.

Landscapes: Shoot in A-dep or the mountain picture mode for precise focusing of entire photo. To make a landscape interesting, frame your scene using natural items. For instance, if there is a colorful tree by a pond, position the tree on the side and top of your photo with the pond in the rest of it. The tree is making a natural frame around the pond and brings great beauty and interest to your picture.

Another way to make a scene interesting is to use the 1/3 rule. Divide your picture into three evenly spaced sections: sky, foreground, and middle of the picture; just make sure your horizon is straight.

Always realize that it's okay to break the rules and color outside the lines. I like to try to look at a picture, item, or scene in a way totally different than the rest of the world. This can make for a really interesting photograph. Something as simple as a tree can have a totally different perspective if you take the time to really look at it.

Also, try to portray a feeling or a story with your photo. What do you want the person who is looking at your photo to feel or know?

Practice Your New Skills: Make a photo collage portraying your family. When people look at this, they should be able to get a sense of what your family is all about. Use the portrait mode on your camera, your AV mode, and action mode to have a variety of pictures.

See how many different ways you can take a picture of a tree.

Take architectural pictures; parts of buildings, bridges, doors, fountains, fences, etc.

Take still life pictures such as fruit, books, sports equipment, food, etc. Use the AV mode or the food picture that is in your scene mode.

Take pictures portraying the area of the country where you live. If you live in the South, take photos of cotton, sweet tea, a hot day, or a pickup truck outside a diner.

Take close-ups of nature. Use your flower mode.

Take bird photos.

Take textural photos of tree bark, moss, rocks, bricks, etc. Use your flower mode.

Take action shots. Try panning with your camera; that is, moving your body and your camera together, along with the action. Snap the picture when the item, such as a car, gets in front of you, but continue following after the snap; then shoot the picture without panning. Do the pictures look different?

Take pictures of water--streams, fountains, drips--with different TVs and see how different the pictures are.

See how many ways you can naturally frame a photo.

Take silhouettes. Have your subject stand with the light behind them. Point your camera as if you are focusing on that light and push the shutter button half way down; then with the button still pushed half way, point your camera at the subject and press the shutter all the way down to shoot the photo.

Here is something to work towards. There are stock companies that sell photos to other companies and people all over the world. You can submit photos to these stock companies, and if they like them, they will put them in their portfolio of photographs. People can then log into these companies' web sites, view the photos, and if they like them, they will purchase them from the stock company, who in turn will pay you. Here are a few names of stock companies. Go on-line and check them out.

istockphoto
shutterstock
bigstock

This is a web site you might want to try. It's called Portrait Professional. They take your portraits and make them look like the pros by smoothing out the face and skin, getting rid of blemishes, and other unwanted things.

The web sites listed below take your pictures and put them on canvas and/or other artistic mediums.

Canvas People are the most reasonably priced. Their canvases are thinner but are good quality.

Decorator's Depot cost a little more but the canvases are nicer. They will also frame photos. They do great work.

Art.com can do anything and everything with photos. Check them out.

Walgreens can make anything you can imagine from blankets to coffee cups, mouse pads, and so on. Their prices are good, too.

CHRISTMAS

HOW TO MAKE YOUR CHRISTMAS HOLIDAYS EASY AND MEMORABLE

We all know that the holidays can be quite stressful and, to say the least, mind boggling! As mothers and fathers we want our children and family to have the most magical and memorable holiday we can possibly give them. Here is a guide to help you achieve your holiday goals without being overwhelmed and just plain worn out. Hopefully, with these tips you can have glorious holidays and, at the same time, enjoy every magical moment.

Let's start with presents. I chose this because if we don't wait till the last minute to purchase them, we won't get caught up in the Christmas rush and traffic and go broke as the holidays approach.

I like to start buying my gifts in January, or at least keep my eyes open for bargains and purchases that I know someone will love. I find that if I buy throughout the year, my budget doesn't take such a hit, and I also save a lot of money by purchasing items that are on sale. Also, don't forget gift cards.

When you buy groceries, go to the gift card section and buy a gift card. This adds little to your grocery bill, versus buying them all in December. These make great stocking stuffers and good Dirty Santa gifts.

Next, let's talk about making personal items for your loved ones. I love to make photo books online and also photo gifts such as calendars and other such items. There are all sorts of things you can craft that will really make your holidays personal: ornaments, cookbooks, vinyl gifts, woodworking, soaps, candles, sewing. Just look on Pinterest; the ideas are endless.

Whatever your hobbies and talents, it's great to give your gifts a personal touch. The only catch with this is, if you wait till October to start making your gifts, it really makes you stressed out and tired. Give yourself a deadline, start early, and get this done before the end of summer. Also, you can save a lot of money on line with sales and deals from different web sites.

Okay, now that we have gotten the gifts purchased and made, we can start thinking of cooking. I like to make and freeze casseroles for the holidays so that if unexpected company shows up or I'm just too busy to cook, I can pull a pan out of the freezer, and we have a wonderful home-cooked meal.

A casserole can be frozen for at least three months. So starting in mid-September, when you make a casserole, make an extra one and freeze it. This way you don't have to do a lot of planning and cooking at one time, and it makes the task a breeze.

To freeze a casserole, cover with foil and/or plastic wrap and put the dish in the freezer before you cook it.   If it has a cracker or cheese topping, put that on just before you cook it. Also, mid-September is the time to start your Christmas baking. Yep, that's right. You can bake cookies that will freeze up to eight months, and cakes will freeze for six months, and pies for one to two months. If you bake these items now, it will give you time during December to make candy and other items that can't be frozen.

I know at my house there are never enough sugar cookies and chocolate chip cookies to last more than a day or two. So if I make a lot of them ahead of time, I always have a surplus just waiting to be enjoyed. You can also make your neighbors homemade cakes and cookies to wish them a Merry Christmas. I know if I wait, sometimes that is the thing that gets put to the side and reluctantly never happens.

Now our presents are bought, our baking and cooking are done, so what's next? Let's think about wrapping our gifts. Try to get all your gifts wrapped before November. There have been some years when I would be up until three in the morning on Christmas Eve trying to get all the presents wrapped. There is nothing more miserable than to be stuck with this task when you are ready to go to bed.

Also, there is nothing prettier than a Christmas tree with beautiful presents underneath. I like to use big, beautiful packages with pretty bows to decorate around the house.

Next on the list are the Christmas cards. I like to pick out a great family picture and make my cards online. This is inexpensive and gives such a personal touch to the cards. Just a few clicks and your cards are done. They can be picked up at the drug store or sent to you in the mail. Get creative with your pictures and "wow" everyone with your one-of-a kind card. Make sure you have your cards addressed and ready to go by November.

Okay, Thanksgiving is over, and we are feeling great about Christmas because we are so prepared. Now it is time to decorate. We decorate the weekend after Thanksgiving. I know some people do it before this. If you do, kudos; you are ready to enjoy your holidays. If you are like me, then let's get busy!!

I like to put all my decorations for a particular room in one or two boxes and label them "den" or "kitchen." This way you can pull the box out of storage and know where to take it, and you're ready to start decorating. This simple tip really does save a lot of time.

We buy a real tree every year and also have a few artificial trees. I buy fresh wreaths because they smell great and don't take up valuable storage space. I usually get them at one of the "big box" stores when they are on sale so it's not a big expense.

I change my decorations a little each year, but for the most part, things go in the same places. This way I don't have to do too much thinking when I deck the halls. The process is quick and painless. I also have pictures on the computer that I can click on, and all my great, or not so great, ideas come flooding back to me.

Remember, to make a big impact in a room use large items like garlands, wreaths, big trees, small trees, quilts, etc., and your house will look festive and put together and not just thrown together. If you have a lot of small items, they don't make an impact, and it just means more time pulling everything out of the boxes and more time putting everything back.

I like to have a photo album laying on the coffee table with pictures of Christmases past in it. Everyone enjoys looking at this. I like to put old photos and old art work of the kids in frames and put them out also.

Now we are finally ready to get down to the real fun and meaning of Christmas. Since you have all the basics done, you can actually enjoy your family and activities all through the season. When the kids were small, we always had a birthday party for Jesus. This helped them to realize the true meaning of Christmas.

We had another day when I got out the craft boxes for them to make Christmas ornaments for the tree. Today I have a whole tree just dedicated to those ornaments. I was really surprised at the different ideas they came up with. Of course we had to decorate a gingerbread house and bake sugar cookies. I know we have some in the freezer, but this is the time to let the kids get in the kitchen and have fun. The cookies all get eaten when they come out of the oven anyway!

I would give the kids special chores to do to earn money so they could buy their siblings, grandparents, and parents presents. I think it's important to teach the kids how to show appreciation to the ones they love by offering them a gift from the heart. By working for them, it made each child really proud of what they had chosen for each person on their list. They could buy the gifts or buy the supplies to make them a gift. Either way, they put a lot of thought into this and learned how to give and not just receive.

Last, but not least, we always worked with a Christmas Charity to help others receive a wonderful holiday, and of course we were the ones who received the blessing for doing so.

MY CHRISTMAS HELPER
January

As you put away your Christmas decorations, think about what you will need for next year, and buy it now while it's on sale: lights, garland, wrapping paper, bows, ribbon, tins for goodies, etc.

Start looking and planning for the gifts you are going to buy this year.

JANUARY

1.
2.
3.
4.
5.
6.
7.
8.
9.
10.
11.
12.
13.
14.
15.

Keep a list of what you buy so that you don't forget—and where you put (hide) it.

LIST OF SUPPLIES I NEED TO MAKE MY GIFTS:

1.
2.
3.
4.
5.
6.
7.
8.
9.
10.
11.
12.
13.
14.
15.
16.
17.
18.
19.
20.

LIST OF ITEMS I WOULD LIKE TO MAKE:

1.

2.

3.

4.

5.

6.

7.

8.

9.

10.

11.

12.

SIZES OF MY FAMILY:

1.

2.

3.

4.

5.

6.

7.

8.

9.

10.

11.

12.

13.

14.

15.

LIST OF MEALS TO COOK AND FREEZE—AUGUST

1.

2.

3.

4.

5.

6.

7.

8.

9.

10.

11.

12.

13.

14.

15.

LIST OF CHRISTMAS BAKING THAT I CAN FREEZE–AUGUST

1.

2.

3.

4.

5.

6.

7.

8.

9.

10.

11.

12.

13.

14.

15.

MEALS I HAVE FROZEN
SEPTEMBER

1.

2.

3.

4.

5.

6.

7.

8.

9.

10.

11.

12.

13.

14.

15.

GOODIES I HAVE BAKED AND FROZEN—SEPTEMBER

1.

2.

3.

4.

5.

6.

7.

8.

9.

10.

11.

12.

13.

14.

15.

CHRISTMAS CARD LIST WITH ADDRESSES—OCTOBER

1.

2.

3.

4.

5.

6.

7.

8.

9.

10.

CARD LIST, CONT'D

11.

12.

13.

14.

15.

16.

17.

18.

19.

20.

21.

CARD LIST, CONT'D

22.

23.

24.

25.

26.

27.

28.

29.

30.

31.

32.

A YEAR OF TEACHING IDEAS
January

Health and Nutrition
Digestive System
Egyptians
Snow
Matter: solids, liquids, and gas
Africa

Spelling list:

acid	exercise	liquid
ancient	fats	meat
blizzard	flake	milk
boil	food	mummy
bread	fruit	pyramid
cheese	gas	queen
chew	gods	river
cold	grain	ski
cow	healthy	slave
dairy	ice	sled
diet	intestine	snow
eat	king	steam

stomach   tomb   water
swallow   vapor

Activities:

Draw and color the food pyramid.

Come up with a better food plan for your family.

Create an exercise program for the whole family.

Find out how many calories and grams of fat fast food has in it.

Teach your children how to cook.

Learn fractions while you cook.

Learn how to add fractions.

Go shopping for groceries, and see if you can stay on budget.

Use coupons while shopping.

Build a pyramid with sugar cubes or legos.

Wear make-up like an Egyptian.

Make home-made paper.

Make scrolls.

Make up your own hieroglyphics.

Study King Tut and Cleopatra.

Make a map of Africa; put Egypt on it and the Nile.

Play in the snow.

Show how snow is a solid; melt it, and it's a liquid; boil it, and it's a gas. If you don't have snow, use an ice cube.

Make snow cones.

Cut out snowflakes.

Make bird feeders; pinecones, peanut butter, and bird seed, then hang in the trees.

Make a snow globe.

Look for animal tracks in the snow and figure out what kind of animal it is.

Go to the zoo and pretend that you are on an African Safari.

Books to Read:

"See Inside Your Body" by Katie Daynes and Colin King.

"Me and My Amazing Body" by Joan Sweeney and Anette Cable.

"Inside Your Outside: All about the Human Body" by Tish Rabe and Aristides Ruiz.

"What is the World Made Of? All About Solid, Liquids, and Gases" by Kathleen Weidner Zoehfeld and Paul Meisel.

"It's Disgusting and We Ate It" by James Solheim.

"The Busy Body Book: A Kids Guide to Fitness" by Lizzy Rockwell.

"My First Human Body Book" by Patricia J. Wynne and Donald M. Silver.

"The Magic School Bus: A Journey into the Human Body" by The Young Scientists' Club.

"Emerils, There's a Chef in My World! Recipes that Take You Places" by Emeril Lagasse.

"Adventures in Ancient Egypt (Good Times Travel Agency)" by Linda Bailey and Bill Slaven.

"Hieroglyphs From A to Z: A Rhyming Book with Ancient Egyptian Stencils For Kids" by Peter Manuelian.

"Magic Tree House Fact Tracker #3: Mummies and Pyramids" by Mary Pope Osborne, Will Osborne, and Sal Murdocca.

"Mummies in the Morning (Magic Tree House, No.3)" by Mary Pope Osborne and Sal Murdoccoa.

"Africa Is Not a Country" by Margy Burns Knight and Anne Sibley O'Brien.

"Jambo Means Hello: Swahili Alphabet Book" by Muriel Feelings and Tom Feelings.

"Safari So Good! All About African Wildlife (Cat in the Hat's Learning Library)" by Bonnie Worth, Aristides Ruiz, Joe Mathieu.

"The Gift of the Sun: A Tale from South Africa" by Dianne Stewart and Jude Daly.

"We All Went on Safari" by Laurie Krebs and Julia Caims.

"The Story of Snow: The Science of Winter's Wonder" by Mark Cassino.

"The Secret Life of a Snowflake: An Up-Close Look at the Art and Science of Snowflakes" by Kenneth Libbrecht.

"Snowflake" Bentley by Jacqueline Briggs Martin and Mary Azarian.

"Animals in Winter" by Henrietta Bancraoft and Richard B. Van Gelder and Helen K. Davie.

"The Snow Globe Family" by Jame O'Connor and S. D. Schindler.

A YEAR OF TEACHING IDEAS
February

Presidents
Recycling
The Circulatory System
Greeks
Greece

Spelling Words:

adore
alphabet
arteries
Athens
athletic
beat
blood
candy
card
chocolate
citizen
compete
cute

defeat
democratic
false
game
garbage
goddess
Greek
heart
hero
idle
island
love
mulch

president   send
pump   shield
receive   sweet
recycle   valentine
reduce   veins
reuse   war
runner   warrior

Activities:

Make valentines.

Start a recycle center in your home.

Have a special valentine breakfast or dinner.

Bake a heart-shaped cake or heart-shaped cookies.

Have a family Olympics.

Cook some Greek food and wear togas to dinner.

Learn the Greek alphabet.

Learn about the different Greek Gods.

Rent some old and new Greek movies, make popcorn and baklava, and have movie night.

Research your favorite presidents.

Make a map of Greece and the Greek Isles. Use a brown paper grocery bag to make it look old.

Books to Read:

"The Children's Homer: The Adventures of Odysseus and the Tale of Troy" by Padraic Colum.

"Woodrow for President" by Cheryl Shaw Barnes and Peter W. Barnes.

"What Presidents Are Made Of" by Hanoch Piven.

"Recycle! A Handbook for Kids" by Gail Gibbons.

"Smash! Mash! Crash! There Goes the Trash! by Barbara Odanaka.

"Classical Kids: An Activity Guide to Life in Ancient Greece and Rome" by Laurie Carlson.

"Greece and Rome" by Laurie Carlson.

"I Wonder Why Greeks Built Temples--and Other Questions About Ancient Greece" by Fiona MacDonald.

"Great Greeks: Fun Poems for Kids About Ancient Greece" by Paul Perro.

"The Librarian Who Measured the Earth" by Kathryn Lasky and Kevin Hawkes.

"Magic Tree House Fast Tracker #10 Ancient Greece and the Olympics."

"The Adventures of An Aluminum Can: A Story About Recycling" by Alison Indes and Mark Chambers.

"Recycling" by Alison Indes and Mark Chambers.

"The Adventures of a Plastic Bottle" by Alison Indies and Pete Whitehead.

"Michael Recycle" by Ellie Bethel and Alexander Colombo.

"The Heart: All About Our Circulatory System and More!" by Seymour Simon.

"The Illiad" by Homer.

"The Odysee" by Homer.

"George Washington's Cows" by David Small.

"A Life Like Mine: How Children Live Around the World" by DK Publishing.

A YEAR OF TEACHING IDEAS
March

Benjamin Franklin
Clouds, weather, wind
Romans
Inventions
Eyes
Italy

Spelling Words:

airplane	fire	politics
ambassador	focus	post office
artist	heat	pupil
bath	insurance	rain
bifocals	inventor	Rome
burn	iris	sign
cloud	kite	soldier
cold	lash	stamp
column	letter	storm
conquer	light bulb	stove
emperor	lions	sunny
empire	look	telephone
eye	pasta	tower

Activities:

Build and fly your own kite.

Make cup or tin can phones. You will need two paper or plastic cups, or two tin cans, and at least ten feet of string. Poke a hole in the bottom of each cup or tin can--large enough to insert the string--then tie a knot in the string. Stretch string as far as it will go; now talk into the cups. Kids love this.

Make paper airplanes.

Go to an airport.

Make pasta and Italian bread for dinner.

Make Italian Cream Cake.

Write letters to your friends and relatives.

Learn Morse Code.

Learn your Roman numerals.

Books to Read:

"Tiger, Tiger" by Lynne Reid Banks.

"I Wonder Why Romans Wore Togas" by Fiona MacDonald.

"Classical Kids: An Activity Guide to Life in Ancient Greece and Rome" by Laurie Carlson.

"The Flyer Flew! The Invention of the Airplane" by Lee Sulllivan.

"Leonardo da Vinci" by Diane Stanley.

"Amazing Leonardo da Vinci Inventions You Can Build" by Maxine Anderson.

"Ben and Me" by Robert Lawson.

"A Life Like Mine: How Children Live Around the World" by DK Publishing.

"Not for Parents, Rome: Everything You Ever Wanted to Know" by Lonely Planet.

"Not for Parents, Venice" by Lonely Planet.

"Not for Parents, Florence" by Lonely Planet.

"Not for Parents, Europe" by Lonely Planet.

"Children's' Book: About Countries" by Brian Cliette.

"Clouds (Let's-Read-and-Find-Out Science 1)" by Anne Rockwell and Frane Lessac.

"Feel the Wind" by Dorros and Arthur Durros.

"What Will the Weather Be?" by Lynda Dewitt and Carolyn Croll.

"Weather Words and What They Mean" by Gail Gibbons.

"The Cloud Book" by Tonie dePaola.

"Helen Keller: Courage in the Dark" by Johanna Hurwitz.

"Ben Franklin and the Magic Squares" by Frank Murphy and Richard Walz.

"Listen Up! Alexander Graham Bell's Talking Machine" by Monica Kulling.

"Eat My Dust! Henry Ford's First Race" by Monica Kulling and Richard Walz.

"This is Venice" by Miroslav Sasek.

"This is Rome" by Miroslav Sasek.

A YEAR OF TEACHING IDEAS
April

Middle Ages
Plants
George Washington
Gardening
England
Worms
American Revolution

Spelling Words:

activities	garden
British	grow
castle	harvest
compost	herb
country	king
crown	kingdom
dirt	knight
England	leader
farmer	leaf
father	leaves
feed	London
founding	mulch

officer
palace
peasant
pick
plant
president
queen
revolution
root
seed

soil
soldier
sprout
vegetable
village
water
weed
worm

Begin a compost pile.

Start a vegetable garden (see garden guide).

Grow herbs in a window.

Start a worm farm.

Visit a plant nursery.

Go to a strawberry farm and pick strawberries.

Make homemade strawberry jam.

Visit Mount Vernon.

Take photos or make drawings of your seeds'germination and label them.

Visit a farm--one organic and one regular.

Research different ways to fertilize your garden.

Make crowns.

Make a family coat of arms.

Make shields and swords.

Dress like royalty; have a banquet with roast chicken, bread, roasted vegetables; and eat with your hands.

Draw the British flag.

Make a map of England.

Get baby chickens from a local feed and seed store.

Build a chicken coop.

Books to Read:

"George vs George: The American Revolution as Seen from Both Sides" by Rosalyn Schanzer.

"George Washington's Cows" by David Small.

"Compost, by Gosh" by Michelle Eva Portman.

"Out and About at the Dairy Farm" by Andy Murphy.

"A Fairy in a Dairy" by Lucy Nolan.

"Where Do Chicks Come From?" by Amy E. Sklansky.

"The Year at Maple Hill Farm" by Alice and Martin Provensen.

"It's Disgusting, and We Ate It" by James Solheim.

"Yucky Worms" by Vivian French and Jessica Ahlberg.

"What Do Roots Do?" by Kathleen V. Kudlinski.

"The American Revolution for Kids: A History With 21 Activities," (For Kids Series) by Janis Herbert, grades 4-6.

"Liberty--How the Revolutionary War Began" by Lucille Penner.

"Meet George Washington" by Joan Heilbroner.

"Nature Anatomy: The Curious Parts and Pieces of the Natural World" by Julia Rothman.

"Rush Revere and the American Revolution" by Rush Limbaugh, ages 9-13.

"George Washington Spymaster: How the Americans Out Spied the British and Won the Revolutionary War" by Thomas B. Allen, ages 10-up, grades 5-up.

"The Scarlet Stockings Spy (Tales of Young Americans) by Trinka Hakes Noble and Robert Papp, ages 6-up, grades 1-4.

"Independent Dames: What You Knew About the Women and Girls of the American Revolution," grades 1-5, ages 6-10.

"Katie's Trunk" by Ann Turner and Ronald Himler, ages 5-8, grades K-3.

"Not for Parents London: Everything You Ever Wanted to Know (Lonely Planet Not For Parents London) by Lonely Planet, ages 8-12.

"The Story of London" by Richard Brassey, grades 4-up.

"This is Britain" by Miroslav Sasek, grades 4-12.

"Dodsworth in London (A Dodsworth Book) by Tim Egan, grades 2-5.

"The Vegetables We Eat" by Gail Gibbons.

"From Seed to Plant" by Gail Gibbons.

"Series—Medieval World" by Crabtree Publishing, ages 10-up, grades 5-up.

"You Wouldn't Want to Live in the Middle Ages" by Fiona MacDonald, Jacqueline Morley (The Danger Zone).

"The Sword in the Tree (Trophy Chapter Book)" by Clyde Robert Bulla and Bruce Bowles, grades 3-7.

A YEAR OF TEACHING IDEAS
May

Flowers
Animals
Nervous System
Renaissance
France
Leonardo daVinci

Spelling List

animal	helicopter
art	horse
artist	hurt
body	leaf
culture	leaves
elephant	machine gun
fashion	mammal
feel	monkey
flower	museum
France	nerve
French	pain

painter
Paris
petal
piston
pollen
pollenate
rebirth
sculptor
species

spine
stamen
stem
tank
tiger
touch
village
zebra

Activities:

Dissect a flower.

Get some white carnations and put them in different glasses with different shades of food color and watch the flowers change from white to a color. (Demonstrates how flowers absorb water).

Plant a flower garden, window box, and/or flower pots.

Go to the zoo, take a journal, and write down the animals you see and where they are from and other information of interest. Now make a book with your info. Also, take pictures of each animal to put in your book.

Make May baskets (baskets with homemade goodies and pretty flowers) and put on your neighbors', friends', and families' door steps. Ring the doorbell then run and hide. This is a forgotten tradition that is fun for everyone!

Visit a working farm.

Paint on canvas and make your own masterpiece.

Buy clay and sculpt.

Have a French breakfast with croissants, hot chocolate, butter and jam.

Make a Monte Cristo sandwich.

Plant some lavender in a pot and keep it outside where you sit or beside your door. It has a wonderful aroma.

Dry some lavender and make sachets for your clothes or linen drawers or closet. It makes everything smell fresh.

Learn French.

Books to Read:

"Amazing Leonardo da Vinci Inventions You Can Build Yourself" by Maxine Anderson.

"The Secret Garden" by Frances Burnett.

"Leonardo da Vinci" by Diane Stanley.

"My Body" by Patty Carratello.

"Me and My Amazing Body" by Joan Sweeney and Anette Cable.

"The Magic School Bus: A Journey into the Human Body" by the Young Scientists Club.

"My First Human Body Book (Dover Children's Science Books)" by Patricia J. Wynne and Donald M. Silver.

"Museum ABC" by Metropolitan Museum of Art.

"See Inside Your Body" by Katie Daynes and Colin King.

"Zoology for Kids: Understanding and Working with Animals, with 21 Activities (For Kids Series)" by Josh Hestermann and Bethanie Hestermann.

"Not for Parents, Paris: Everything You Ever Wanted to Know (Lonely Planet Not for Parents) by Lonley Planet.

"Flower Garden" by Eve Bunting and Kathryn Hewit, ages 3-7.

"Sunflower House" by Eve Bunting and Kathryn Hewit, ages 4-7.

"Getting to Know France and French (Getting to Know Series)" by Nicola Wright and Kim Wooley, ages 8-12.

"Find Out About France: Learn French Words and Phrases and About Life in France (Find Out About Books)" by Duncan Crosbie.

"Come With Me to Paris (City Series)" by Gloria Fowler and Min Heo, ages 2-up.

"Series—Renaissance World" by Crabtree Publishing:

"The Renaissance in Europe" by Lynn Elliott.
"Painting in the Renaissance" by Lynn Elliott.
"Science in the Renaissance" by Lisa Mullins.
"Exploration in the Renaissance" by Lynn Elliott.
"Great Ideas of the Renaissance" by Trudee Romanek, ages 10-up, grades 5-up.
"Outrageous Women of the Renaissance" by Vicki Leon.

"The Renaissance (History Open Windows)" by Jane Shuter, grades 3-6.

"The Story of Napoleon" by Henriette Elizabeth Marshall, ages 10-12, grades 5-7.

A YEAR OF TEACHING

June

Insects
The Ocean
Pirates
Reformation
Australia
Blackbeard
Black Bart
Sir Francis Drake
Calico Jack
Anne Booney
Mary Read

Spelling Words:

anchor	current
antenna	deck
beach	doctrine
beard	dolphin
church	fish
comb	flag
crab	floor

hive	sail
honey	salt
insect	sand
island	shark
kangaroo	shell
moon	ship
ocean	stinger
octopus	sword
patch	tide
pool	wave
raid	whale
reef	wings
reform	worker

Activities:

Catch and classify as many insects as you can; take their pictures, and after observing them for a day or two, let them go.

Fill a container with water; now fill another container with sand and place in the middle of the water-filled container. It will be like an island. Very carefully scoop up part of an ant hill and put on the island. Watch and observe the ants. You will be entertained for hours. If there are no ant hills where you live, you can actually order an ant farm.

Visit a bee keeper.

Make peanut butter and honey sandwiches.

Go to the beach.

Make a collection of shells.

Catch sand crabs at night on the beach.

Go crabbing off a pier at the bay or beach. Get a string or crab net and tie bacon fat or a chicken neck to it. Lower bait into the water and wait for the crabs to find it and attach themselves to it. Slowly pull them up to a waiting net.

Go on a cruise and see the dolphins and fish.

Go fishing off a pier, at the shore, or even go deep sea fishing.

Dissect a fish.

Make pirate hats, patches, and cardboard swords, and play pirates.

Make a pirate map and hide a treasure for the kids to find by using the map.

Let the kids make pirate maps out of old grocery bags. Tear the paper bags into large pieces. Have an adult burn the edges of the bag to make it look old. Let the children use this to make their maps.

Get a large cardboard box and make a pirate ship out of it.

Go to an aquarium.

Have movie night and watch Pirates of the Caribbean.

Learn how to use a compass.

Draw a map of Australia.

Catch lightning bugs (fireflies).

Books to Read:

"Pirateology" by Dugald A. Steer.

"Latitude and Longitude" by Rebecca Aberg.

"What If You Met a Pirate?" by Jan Adkins.

"Clean Sea: Story of Rachel Carson" by Carol Hilgartner.

"Are We There Yet?" by Alison Lester (a book about Australia).

"The Magic School Bus Inside a Beehive" by Joanna Cole and Bruce Degen.

"Are You a Bee?" by Judy Allen (one in a series of insect books).

"The Honey Makers" by Gail Gibbons.

"Blackbeard, the Pirate King" by J. Patrick Lewis.

"How I Became a Pirate" by Melinda Long.

"Ocean Soup: Tide-Pool Poems" by Stephen R. Swinburne and Bruce Hiscock.

"An Octopus Is Amazing" by Patricia Lauber and Holly Keller.

"What Lives in a Shell?" by Kathleen Weidner Zoehfel and Helen K. Davie.

"The Magic School Bus On the Ocean Floor" by Joanna Cole and Bruce Degen.

"What's Under the Sea?" by Sophy Tahta and Stuart Trotter.

"Insectigations, 40 Hands-on Activities to Explore the Insect World" by Cindy Blobaum.

"Sea Queens. Women Pirates Around the World" by Jane Yolen and Christine Joy Pratt, grades 4-6.

"Courage and Conviction: Chronicles of Reformation Church (History Lives Series)" by Brandon Withrow and Mindy Withrow.

"Brilliant Brits: Henry VIII" by Richard Brassey, ages 7-9.

"Thunderstorm in Church" by Vernon Louise; a book about Martin Luther, ages 9-up.

A YEAR OF TEACHING IDEAS
July

Industrial Revolution
Muscular System
Electricity
Declaration of Independence
The Bill of Rights
The Constitution
Betsy Ross
Germany

Spelling Words:

America
beautiful
blue
brave
celebrate
convention
electric

fight
flag
holiday
independence
justice
land
leader

liberty	star
machine	states
meeting	stripe
muscle	switch
nation	united
national	war
pride	white
religion	write

Activities:

Have a Fourth of July parade in your neighborhood.

Have a Fourth of July party.

Go to your local fireworks celebration.

Have your children create their ideal country. They will need to write their country's constitution, create a flag, have a national bird and flower; and if they are really creative, write their national anthem.

Paint or draw the American Flag.

Learn the 50 states and their capitals.

Get a map of the United States and highlight all the places you have been. Put flags or stickers on the places you would like to go.

Have a *states and capitals tournament*. Select two players and sit them at a table side by side. Put a spoon between the two players. Name a state; the player who knows the capital first--and is the first one to pick up the spoon--wins the point. If they pick up the spoon and don't know the answer, they are penalized a point. At the end the player with the most points wins, then they can challenge the next player in line.

Make an apple pie, and on the top crust, with food color, paint a flag, stars, patchwork quilt, whatever!! Then bake.

Learn some German words.

Go on line and learn how to make a potato powered light bulb or clock.

Make dinner with my recipes for German food in the recipe section of this book.

Books:

"The Declaration of Independence" by Elaine Londau.

"Will You Sign Here, John Hancock" by Jean Fritz.

"Shh! We're Writing the Constitution" by Jean Fritz.

"Charged Up: The Story of Electricity" by Jacqui Bailey and Matthew Lilly.

"The Magic School Bus Jumping into Electricity."

"Red, White, and Blue" (Penguin Young Readers, L3).

"The Story of the Star Spangled Banner" by Patricia A. Pingry and Nancy Munger.

"Liberty Lee's Tale of Independence" by Cheryl Shaw.

"Sweet Land of Liberty (Ellis the Elephant)" by Callista Gingrich and Susan Arciero.

"Our 50 States" by Lynne Cheney and Robin Preiss Glasser.

"Switch on, Switch Off" by Melvin Berger and Carolyn Croll.

"My First Human Body Book" by Patricia J. Wynne and Donald M Silver.

"My Body" by Patty Carratello.

"Me and My Amazing Body" by Joan Sweeney and Anette Cable.

"Inside Your Outside: All About the Human Body" by Tish Rabe and Aristides Ruiz (Cat and the Hat Series).

"The Busy Body Book: A Kid's Guide to Fitness" by Lizzy Rockwell.

"All About America: The Industrial Revolution" by Hilarie N. Staton, ages 9-12.

"The Industrial Revolution for Kids (For Kids Series)" by Cheryl Mullenback, ages 9-up, grades 4-up.

"Betsy Ross: Patriot of Philadelphia (Red Feather Books)" by Judith St George and Sasha Meret, grades 4-7, ages 8-12.

"Germany: Amazing Pictures and Fun Facts (Kid Kongo Travel the World Series) (Volume 8)" by Kid Kongo, ages 5-12.

"Mercedes and the Chocolate Pilot" by Margo Theis Raven.

"Truce: The Day the Soldiers Stopped Fighting" by Jim Murphy, grades 3-7.

A YEAR OF TEACHING IDEAS
August

Solar System
Astronauts
Shakespeare
Airplanes
Rockets
Space Shuttle
Space Station
Spain
Civil War

Spelling Words:

acting
actor
astronomer
astronaut
atmosphere
comet
dream
Earth
falling

galaxy
gaze
gravity
Mars
Mercury
meteor
milky way
Moon
night
perform

planet
planetarium
play
Pluto
rings
rocket
Saturn
Shakespeare
shuttle
sky
space

stage
stars
station
summer
sun
telescope
theater
Uranus
Venus
writer

Activities:

Put on a play. Have your children write their version of a Shakespearean play and then act it out.

Put blankets and pillows in the yard at night and gaze at the stars. Look online to see when a meteor shower will be in your area.

Get the "star app" for your cell phone. You can hold the phone up towards the sky, and it will tell you what star constellation you are looking at. It's really neat!

Get a telescope and look at the planets.

Go to a planetarium.

Make a model of the solar system out of styrofoam balls.

Put glow-in-the-dark stars on your kid's ceiling.

Let the kids draw and decorate the planets on poster board (both sides) and hang them from their ceilings.

Make a rocket from a cardboard refrigerator container.

Make a space helmet out of a square cardboard box. Cut the flaps off the top and make a hole in one side.

Have a movie night and watch Civil War movies.

Make a rocket out of a coke bottle.

Make paper airplanes in different ways and see which design flies best, highest, longest, etc.

Go to an airport and watch planes take off and land.

Have a pretend bull fight. Red table cloth--El Toro!!

Make Spanish food.

Dance.

Draw maps that show the division of the Nation, Mason Dixon line, North and South.

Go to a Civil War re-enactment, a battlefield, or museum.

Books:

"The Flyer Flew! The Invention of the Airplane" by Lee Sullivan.

"The Planets in Our Solar System" (Let's-Read-and-Find-Out 2).

"What's Out There? A Book About Space." (Reading Railroad) by Lynn Wilson and Paige Billin-Frye.

"Astronaut Handbook" by Meaghan McCarthy.

"National Geographic Readers: Planets" by Elizabeth Carney.

"The Shakespeare Stealer" by Gary Blackwood.

"Beautiful Stories From Shakespeare for Children" by E. Nesbit.

"Soccer World: Spain: Explore the World Through Soccer" by Ethan Zohn and David Rosenberg," ages 7-9, grades 2-4.

"Adventures of Don Quixote (Dover's Children's Thrift Classics) Abridged Edition" by Argentina Palacios, ages 8-14, grades 3-8.

"The Story of Ferdinand" by Munro Leaf and Robert Lawson (about a bull in Spain).

"Find Out About Spain: Learn Spanish Words and Phrases and About Life in Spain (Find-Out-About-Series)" by Duncan Crossbie, ages 8-12.

"The Children's Civil War (Civil War America)" by James Marten, grades 6-up.

"The Boys' War: Confederate and Union Soldiers Talk About the Civil War" by Jim Murphy, grades 5-7.

"You Wouldn't Want to be a Civil War Soldier" by Thomas Ratliff.

"The Civil War for Kids: A History With 21 Activities (For Kids Series)" by Janis Herbert, ages 9-up, grades 4-up.

"Bard of Avon: The Story of William Shakespeare" by Diane Stanley and Peter Vennema, ages 6-10, grades 1-5.

"The Magic School Bus Lost in the Solar System" by Joanna Cole and Bruce Degen.

"Max Goes to the Space Station" by Jeffrey Bennett and Michael Carroll.

"The International Space Station (Let's-Read-and-Find-Out, Science 2)" by Franklyn M. Branley and True Kelley, grades K-4.

"Mousetronaut: Based On a (partially) True Story (Paula Wiseman Books)" by Mark Kelly and C. F. Payne.

"Floating in Space (Let's-Read-and-Find-Out, Science 2)" by Franklyn M. Branley and True Kelley, grades K-4.

A YEAR OF TEACHING IDEAS
September

Pompeii
Rocks
Earth
Volcanoes
Hawaii and Pearl Harbor
Fossils
Dinosaurs

Spelling Words:

active
ashes
attack
bomb
canoe
coconut
dancer
dinosaur
dock
dormant
earth

explode
fire
flow
fossil
geography
Hawaii
inactive
island
Japanese
kayak
lava
layer

navy
officer
palm
Pearl Harbor
pilot
pineapple
rock
sailor
ship

snorkel
surf
surprise
torch
tropical
uniform
volcano
war

Activities:

Go rock collecting.

With the parent's help and safety glasses, break open rocks to see the beauty they have inside.

Learn the different layers of the earth, then make salt bottle designs to show how soil layers look underground. Get a large container of salt. Separate the salt into different pie pans and--with colored chalk--rub the salt until it turns color. Do as many colors as you desire. Layer the different colors of salt into the bottle. A bottle with a lid is best if you want to keep it.

After the layers are all in the bottle, take a skewer or wire and insert *inside* on the side of the bottle. Try to make it all the way to the bottom of the bottle, then gently pull up and straight out. Do this around entire bottle and watch the beautiful designs appear.

Blow up a balloon and put paper mache on entire balloon surface, except a tiny hole on top. Let dry. Pop balloon at the tiny hole and then paint your earth.

Make a working volcano.

Have a luau. Make lei's to put around your neck.

Hula dance.

Eat a fresh pineapple.

Slice off the top of the pineapple. Place cut side in sandy potting soil (just barely cover cut side) and grow a pineapple.

Make a fossil.

Search for fossils.

Learn about the different kinds of dinosaurs.

Have movie night and watch movies about dinosaurs, Pompeii, and Pearl Harbor.

Books:

"Pearl Harbor: Ready to Read Level 3" by Stephen Krensky and Larry Day," ages 6-9, grades 1-4.

"The Attack on Pearl Harbor: An Interactive History Adventure" by Allison Lassieur, ages 8-12.

"The Mystery in Hawaii: Our 50th State (Real Kids, Real Places)" by Carole Marsh.

"Baby Honu's Incredible Journey" by Tammy Yee, ages 2-6.

"Dirtmeister's Nitty Gritty Planet Earth: All About Rocks, Minerals, Fossils, Earthquakes, Volcanoes, and Even Dirt (National Geographic Kids)" by Steve Tomecek and Fred Harper, ages 8-12, grades 3-7.

"National Geographic: Little Kid's First Big Book of Dinosaurs" by Catherine D. Huges and Franco Tempesta, ages 4-8, grades PK-3.

"Act Normal and Don't Tell Anyone About the Dinosaur in the Garden" by Christian Darkin, ages 5-9.

"Read and Find Out Series," grades K-4:
   "Digging Up Dinosaurs" by Aliki.
   "Fossils Tell of Long Ago" by Aliki.
   "Archaeologists Dig for Clues" by Katie Duke.
   "Dinosaur Bones" by Aliki.
   "Let's Go Rock Collecting" by Roma Gans and Holly Keller.

"Pompeii. . . Buried Alive (Step Into Reading)" by Edith Kunhardt.

"You Wouldn't Want to Live in Pompeii; A Volcano Eruption You'd Rather Avoid" by John

Malam, David Salariya, and David Antram, ages 8-up, grades 3-up.

"Vacation Under the Volcano (Magic Tree House No. 13)" by Mary Pope Osborne, ages 6-9, grades 1-4.

"What Was Pompeii?" by Jim O'Conner, Fred Harper, and John Hinderliter, ages 8-12, grades 3-7.

"What Was Pearl Harbor?" by Patricia Brennan, John Mantha, and Tim Tamkinson, ages 8-12, grades 3-7.

"Volcanoes (Let's-Read-and-Find-Out Science 2)" by Franklyn M. Branley and True Kelley.

A YEAR OF TEACHING IDEAS
October

The Age of Discovery
Christopher Columbus
Henry Hudson
Amerigo Vespucci
Leif Ericson
Jacques Cartier
Hernando de Soto
Father Jacques Marquette and Louis Jolliet
Rene-Robert de La Salle
Verrazano
Cabeza de Vaca
Coronada
Tristan de Luna
Trees and Leafs
Monarch butterfly

Spelling Words:

acorn
apple
autumn
bark
bonfire
branch
bright
brisk
butterfly
camp
camping
candy
caramel
chilly
cinnamon
collect
colorful
costume
discover
explore
explorers

fair
fall
falling
festival
flight
football
fright
helmet
hike
hiking
hummingbird
insect
jacket
jack-o-lantern
leaf
leaves
limb
marshmallow
migrate
patch
peanut
pecan

pie	spooky
popcorn	stew
pumpkin	touchdown
rake	treats
raking	tree
scarecrow	trunk
spider	wings

Activities:

Go apple picking.

Make an apple pie.

Roast pumpkin seeds.

Collect leaves and iron between two sheets of wax paper.

Build a fire and make s'mores.

Sprinkle cinnamon in water and simmer all day in a small pot on the stove. It will make your house smell so good.

Make caramel apples.

Look up the history of Halloween--All Hallows Eve.

Make popcorn balls.

Go on a hayride.

Go to a pumpkin patch.

Carve pumpkins.

Have a family football day. Play football outside and have everyone wear their favorite team colors. Have camp stew and chili and homemade goodies. Make a fire outside to sit around, using hay bales for seats, if available. Have treats to roast on the fire. While everyone is together take the family Christmas card picture.

Go hiking and see how many trees you can recognize and which ones are evergreens, deciduous, gymnosperms, angiosperms, conifer, etc.

Make monarch butterflies out of clothes pins and coffee filters, or make them by dabbing globs of paint on a sheet of paper, folding it in half and separating again. Follow the migration patterns of the monarch.

Pick eight of your favorite explorers and study two a week.

Books:

"Tell Me, Tree: All About Trees for Kids" by Gail Gibbons, grades 1-3.

"Draw Write Now" by Marie Hablitzel and Kim Stitzer, a book that teaches you to draw while learning about Christopher Columbus, autumn harvest, and the weather!

"Apples, Apples Everywhere" by Robin Koontz.

"Leaves Fall Down" by Kathie Knerl, ages 4-8.

"Why Do Leaves Change Color?" by Betsy Maestro and Lorretta Krupinski.

"Light and the Glory for Young Readers: 1492-1787 (Discovering Gods Plan for America)" by Peter Marshall, David Manuel, and Anna Wilson Fishel.

"Where Do You Think You're Going, Christopher Columbus?"

"Christopher Columbus' First Voyage to America From the Log of the *Santa Maria*" by Christopher Columbus.

"Explorers of the New World: Discover the Golden Age of Exploration with 22 Projects (Build It Yourself)" by Carla Mooney and Tom Casteel.

<u>You Wouldn't Want to Series</u>, ages 8-up, grades 3-up:

"You Wouldn't Want to Sail with Christopher Columbus: Uncharted Waters You'd Rather Not Cross" by Fiona MacDonald, David Salariya, and David Antram.

"You Wouldn't Want to Explore with Sir Frances Drake" by David Stewart.

"You Wouldn't Want to Explore with Marco Polo" by Jacqueline Marlay, David Salariya, and David Antram.

"You Wouldn't Want to be a Viking Explorer" by Andrew Langley.

"Gotta Go, Gotta Go (Sunburst Books)" by Sam Swope and Sue Riddle, 3-6 years.

"When Butterflies Cross the Sky: The Monarch Butterfly Migration" by Sharon Katz Cooper and Joshua Brunel, ages 5-9, grades 2-3.

"How to Raise Monarch Butterflies: A Step-by-step Guide for Kids (How It Works)" by Carol Paternak, ages 6-12, grades 1-7.

A YEAR OF TEACHING IDEAS
November

American Government
The First Settlers
Indian Tribes in America
First Settlement/Colony of St. Augustine
Roanoke, "The Lost Colony"
Jamestown
Plymouth Colony

Spelling Words:

arrow	election
bake	families
ballot	family
blessings	favorite
Congress	feast
cook	feathers
corn	gobble
delicious	government
democracy	harvest
dinner	homemade

hunting
Indian
pheasant
pilgrim
plentiful
plenty
popcorn
prayer
prepare
rifle
roast
scent

Senate
settlement
settler
simmer
table
thankful
thanks
togetherness
turkey
village
vote

Activities:

Have a mock election. Have someone run for president. Map out a campaign--what are you going to do when you are president, what issues are you for and/or against, etc. Are you democrat or republican and why? Make a speech in front of the family. Have two or more kids running for office; have a debate. Have the family members vote on who they want as their next president. Vote just as we do with a secret ballot.

Re-enact the first Thanksgiving. Dress up like pilgrims and Indians. Have turkey, corn, beans, etc. Enlist the kid's help in preparing the meal, setting the tables, and inviting friends over to participate.

Write your own Thanksgiving play to be the entertainment for your re-enactment.

Learn how to shoot a bow and arrow.

Make an Indian teepee for the kids to play in.

Go canoeing.

Make turkeys out of pinecones. Use these as place card holders for your Thanksgiving table.

Make turkeys out of handprints.

Make placemats for your family's Thanksgiving.

Get a tree branch from outside and put into a flower pot so that it stands up straight. Cut out colorful leaves and punch a hole in the top of each leaf. Thread yarn through each hole and tie in a knot. Put the leaves in a bowl by the tree and let each family member write what they are thankful for and hang it on the tree. Put it in the middle of your dinner table for a great centerpiece and conversation starter.

Books:

"On the Mayflower" by Kate Waters.

"The Story of the Pilgrims" by Katherine Ross.

"My Senator and Me" by Edward M. Kennedy.

"The Very First Americans" by John Herman.

"House Mouse; Senate Mouse; Woodrow for President; Woodrow the White House Mouse," a series by Cheryl Shaw Barnes and Peter W. Barnes.

"Trail of Tears (Step Into Reading Step5)" by Joseph Bruchac, ages 7-9, grades 2-4.

"Exploring Native American Cultures With 25 Great Projects" by Anita Yasuda and Jennifer K. Keller.

"A Day in the Life Series: A Pilgrim Boy; Tapenum's Day; Sarah Morton's Day" by Kate Waters and Russ Kendall, ages 4-8, grades PK-3.

"Rush Revere and the Brave Pilgrims" by Rush Limbaugh.

"Roanoke: Solving the Mystery of the Lost Colony" by Lee Miller.

"The Lost Colony of Roanoke" by Jean Fritz, ages 7-10, grades 2-5.

"Voices in St Augustine" by Jane R. Wood and Elizabeth A. Blacker.

"My America: Our Strange New Land: Elizabeth's Jamestown Colony Diary-Book One; The Starving Time-Book Two; Season of Promise-Book Three" by Patricia Hermes (My America Series) ages 7-10, grades 2-5.

"Surviving Jamestown: The Adventures of Young Sam Collier" by Gail Karwosk and Paul Casale, ages 9-up, grades 4-up.

"Squanto's Journey: The Story of the First Thanksgiving" by Joseph Bruchac and Greg Shed.

"Bury My Heart at Wounded Knee" by Dee Brown.

FUN THINGS TO DO IN DECEMBER

Go to the Christmas parade.

Go to a Christmas cantata.

Have a cookie exchange.

Have a baking day with friends.

Have a tree trimming party.

Make a special day with friends when picking out your Christmas trees--lunch, hayride, tree cutting.

Have a progressive dinner.

Go Christmas caroling.

Help with a charity.

Have a Christmas open house.

Make a day to take your special friends and neighbors their gifts of homemade baked goods.

Take the kids shopping and out to lunch or to the park with a picnic.

Ride around and look at Christmas lights.

Give the kids treats to eat in the car and play or sing Christmas carols as you go.

Have movie nights with all of your favorite Christmas movies, pizza, and goodies.

Go to a nursing home and sing Christmas carols; take the residents a care package of tissues, hard candy, and homemade cards.

Check out your local paper and do some of the fun events planned for your area.

Have a Happy Birthday Jesus Party for your little ones.

Bake sugar cookies with your children.

Make a gingerbread house.

Let your kids make Christmas decorations.

BIBLE DEVOTIONAL BOOKS
FOR THE
WHOLE FAMILY

"God's Wisdom for Little Boys: Character Building Fun from Proverbs" by Jim George, Elizabeth George, and Judy Luenebrink.

"God's Wisdom for Little Girls: Virtues and Fun from Proverbs 31" by Elizabeth George and Judy Luenebrink.

"A Little Girl after God's Own Heart: Learning God's Ways in My Early Days" by Elizabeth George and Judy Luenebrink.

"A Little Boy after God's Own Heart" by Jim George and Judy George.

"The One Year Devotions for Preschoolers" by Crystal Bowman and Elena Kucharik, ages 3-6.

"Grace for the Moment, 365 Devotions for Kids" by Max Lucado, ages 6-10.

"Five-Minute Devotions for Children: Celebrating God's World as a Family" by Pamela Kennedy (fun facts about animals, great simple science, and a devotional).

"More Five-Minute Bible Devotions for Children: Celebrating God's World as a Family" by Pamela Kennedy, Douglas Kennedy, and Amy Wummer.

"Absolutely Awesome and Absolutely Awesome 2" by Michael and Caroline Carroll, ages 8-up (Science and God).

"Fuel: Devotions to Ignite the Faith of Parents and Teens (Focus on the Family Books)" by Joe White.

"Undivided: A Family Devotional: Living For and Not Just With One Another" by Rhonda and Mitchell Owens.

If you like Duck Dynasty, they have a lot of Christian books for fun reading.

"God So Loved the World . . . That He Created Chocolate: 52 Fun and Inspiring

Devotions for Women" by Group Publishing.

Three Books by Ann Voskamp:

"One Thousand Gifts: A Dare to Live Fully Right Where You Are."

"One Thousand Gifts Study Guide: A Dare to Live Fully Right Where You Are."

"One Thousand Gifts Devotional: Reflections on Finding Everyday Graces."

"The One-Year Uncommon Life Daily Challenge" by Tony Dungy and Nathan Whitaker (great for men).

"Conversations With Jesus: 365 Daily Devotions for Teens (Seeking the Heart of God)" by Lisa Cheater.

"The Power of a Praying Teen" by Stormie Omartian.

"Make Every Day Count, Teen Edition" by Max Lucado.

MY FAVORITE SCRIPTURES

<u>Deuteronomy 11:19.</u>

And ye shall teach them, your children, speaking of them when thou sittest in thine house, and when thou walkest by the way, and when thou liest down, and when thou sittest up.

<u>Psalm 118:24.</u>

This is the day the Lord has made; we will rejoice and be glad in it.

<u>1 Chronicles 16:11.</u>

Seek the Lord and his strength; seek his face continually.

<u>Philippians 4:6.</u>

Be careful for nothing; but in everything by prayer and supplication with thanksgiving let your requests be made known to God.

1 Thessalonians 5:17.

Pray without ceasing.

Proverbs 3:6.

In all your ways acknowledge him, and he will make your paths straight.

Proverbs 12:15.

You cannot convince a fool of his folly; only a wise man will accept a rebuke for foolhardiness.

Proverbs 16:2.

A man deep in wickedness will invent "pretty names for sin."

Proverbs 20:7 and 22:6.

Godly parents are a blessing to children and should instruct them in the right way.

Proverbs 20, 23, 31.

Drunkenness is condemned with other severe sins:

Neither the sexually immoral, nor adulterers, nor male prostitutes, nor homosexual offenders, nor thieves, nor the greedy, nor drunkenness, nor slanderers, nor swindlers will inherit the Kingdom of Heaven.

John 16:23-24.

Most assuredly, I say to you whatever you ask the Father in my name He will give you.

1 Thessalonians 5:16-18.

Rejoice always! Pray constantly. Give thanks in everything for this is God's will for you in Christ Jesus.

Philippians 4:6.

Be anxious for nothing, but in everything by prayer and supplication, with thanksgiving, let your requests be made known to God.

Psalm 46:10.

Be still and know that I am God.

<u>Proverbs 16:20.</u>

The one who trusts in the Lord will be happy.

CPSIA information can be obtained
at www.ICGtesting.com
Printed in the USA
LVOW05s0140240517
535631LV00005B/44/P